2726470 WOODWARD, Z. One hundred
         & I. COMᴿˢ   favourite

821.008 AS 9/86
01363

HERTFORDSHIRE LIBRARY SERVICE
Please return this book on or before the
last date shown or ask for it to be renewed

L.32/rev.'81

GW00467701

ONE
HUNDRED
FAVOURITE
POEMS

Also compiled by
Zenka and Ian Woodward

Poems for Fun
Witches' Brew
Poems for Christmas
The Beaver Book of Creepy Verse
Poems That Go Bump in the Night

ONE HUNDRED FAVOURITE POEMS

Compiled by Zenka and
Ian Woodward

Illustrated by Douglas Hall

HUTCHINSON
London Melbourne Sydney Auckland Johannesburg

To
Stefan and Andrea Schäfer
we fondly dedicate
this book of poems

HERTFORDSHIRE
LIBRARY SERVICE
821.008

2726470

Hutchinson Children's Books Ltd
An imprint of the Hutchinson Publishing Group
17–21 Conway Street, London W1P 6JD

Hutchinson Publishing Group (Australia) Pty Ltd
16–22 Church Street, Hawthorn, Melbourne, Victoria 3122, Australia

Hutchinson Group (NZ) Ltd
32–34 View Road, PO Box 40–086, Glenfield, Auckland 10

Hutchinson Group (SA) Pty Ltd
PO Box 337, Bergvlei 2012, South Africa

First published 1985
© In this collection Zenka and Ian Woodward 1985
Illustrations © Douglas Hall 1985

Set in Garamond
Printed and bound in Great Britain by Anchor Brendon Ltd,
Tiptree, Essex

British Library Cataloguing in Publication Data
One hundred favourite poems.
  1. English poetry
  I. Woodward, Zenka   II. Woodward, Ian
  821'.008'09282   PR1175.3
  ISBN 0–09–162470–3

Introduction

Since the title of this anthology speaks for itself, we would just like to say a few words about what we have *not*, rather than what we have, included in the following pages. There were several familiar and popular poems which we would like to have to put in but were unable to because of their length.

Robert Browning's *The Pied Piper of Hamelin* and Longfellow's *The Song of Hiawatha* are perfect examples of what we mean. The first is almost impossible to abbreviate, since each verse is crucial to the overall tale; and even if we were to take just one of the several 'chapters' from the epic *Hiawatha*, then this would still require several pages to accommodate it. So, regrettably, the *very* long popular poem will not be found here.

We have also excluded nursery rhymes, limericks and, by and large, hymns and traditional songs. This is because our theme is one hundred favourite poems and to do it justice we felt we must keep to the narrower definition of poetry.

Finally, a note about the presentation of the poems. To have divided them into various categories, with titles such as 'The Seasons', 'The Countryside' or 'The Sea', would, we think, have detracted from our main purpose. This, quite simply, is to provide in a single volume the very best in children's poetry and it seems quite unnecessary to lump together several poems under a particular subject heading in order to achieve this ambition. The individual poem of excellence speaks for itself, on its own terms.

But, as in all our anthologies, a certain continuity of thought, spirit and adventure runs throughout the book. Any poem you choose at random will be related in some way to the poem immediately before it and to the one following it.

Leonard Clark, who has written the delightful *First Primrose* on page 112, can rightfully take his place alongside such great poets for children as Robert Louis Stevenson, Christina Rossetti, Rudyard Kipling, Walter de la Mare, James Reeves, Ted Hughes and Charles Causley. We single him out for particular mention because we agree with him entirely when he says that children should be accepted for what they are, and be credited with all the powers which they possess in such abundance and variety.

'A good poem for children,' says Leonard Clark, 'must first of all be a good poem, as acceptable to a sensitive and informed adult as to a child.' We sincerely hope that in our personal choice we have brought together a whole treasure trove of such 'good poems'.

Zenka and Ian Woodward

All the world's a stage
(from *As You Like It*)

All the world's a stage,
And all the men and women merely players:
They have their exits and their entrances;
And one man in his time plays many parts,
His acts being seven ages. At first the infant,
Mewling and puking in the nurse's arms.
And then the whining schoolboy, with his satchel,
And shining morning face, creeping like snail
Unwillingly to school. And then the lover,
Sighing like furnace, with a woeful ballad
Made to his mistress' eyebrow. Then a soldier,
Full of strange oaths, and bearded like the pard,
Jealous in honour, sudden and quick in quarrel,
Seeking the bubble reputation
Even in the cannon's mouth. And then the justice,
In fair round belly with good capon lined,
With eyes severe, and beard of formal cut,
Full of wise saws and modern instances;
And so he plays his part. The sixth age shifts
Into the lean and slippered pantaloon,
With spectacles on nose and pouch on side,
His youthful hose well saved, a world too wide
For his shrunk shank; and his big manly voice,
Turning again toward childish treble, pipes
And whistles in his sound. Last scene of all,
That ends this strange eventful history,
Is second childishness and mere oblivion,
Sans teeth, sans eyes, sans taste, sans everything.

William Shakespeare

Solitude

Laugh, and the world laughs with you;
    Weep, and you weep alone;
For the sad old earth must borrow its mirth,
    But has trouble enough of its own.
Sing, and the hills will answer;
    Sigh, it is lost on the air;
The echoes bound to a joyful sound,
    But shrink from voicing care.

Rejoice, and men will seek you;
    Grieve, and they turn and go;
They want full measure of all your pleasure,
    But they do not need your woe.
Be glad, and your friends are many;
    Be sad, and you lose them all –
There are none to decline your nectared wine,
    But alone you must drink life's gall.

Feast, and your halls are crowded;
    Fast, and the world goes by.
Succeed and give, and it helps you live,
    But no man can help you die.
For there is room in the halls of pleasure
    For a large and lordly train,
But one by one we must all file on
    Through the narrow aisles of pain.

Ella Wheeler Wilcox

Good and clever

If all the good people were clever,
    And all clever people were good,
The world would be nicer than ever
    We thought that it possibly could.

But somehow it's seldom or never
    The two hit it off as they should,
The good are so harsh to the clever,
    The clever, so rude to the good!

So friends, let it be our endeavour
    To make each by each understood;
For few can be good, like the clever,
    Or clever, so well as the good.

Elizabeth Wordsworth

Light shining out of darkness

God moves in a mysterious way,
    His wonders to perform;
He plants his footsteps in the sea,
    And rides upon the storm.

Deep in unfathomable mines
    Of never-failing skill,
He treasures up his bright designs,
    And works his sovereign will.

You fearful saints, fresh courage take,
    The clouds you so much dread
Are big with mercy, and shall break
    In blessings on your head.

Judge not the Lord by feeble sense,
    But trust him for his grace;
Behind a frowning providence,
    He hides a smiling face.

His purposes will ripen fast,
    Unfolding every hour;
The bud may have a bitter taste,
    But sweet will be the flower.

Blind unbelief is sure to err,
    And scan his work in vain;
God is his own interpreter,
    And he will make it plain.

William Cowper

The pilgrim

Who would true valour see,
    Let him come hither!
One here will constant be
    Come wind, come weather;
There's no discouragement
Shall make him once relent
His first-avowed intent
    To be a pilgrim.

Whoso beset him round
    With dismal stories,
Do but themselves confound;
    His strength the more is.
No lion can him fright;
He'll with a giant fight;
But he will have a right
    To be a pilgrim.

Hobgoblin, nor foul fiend,
    Can daunt his spirit;
He knows he at the end
    Shall life inherit.
Then, fancies, fly away;
He'll not fear what men say;
He'll labour, night and day,
    To be a pilgrim.

John Bunyan

Peace

My soul, there is a country
    Afar beyond the stars,
Where stands a winged sentry
    All skilful in the wars.
There, above noise and danger,
    Sweet peace sits, crowned with smiles,
And one born in a manger
    Commands the beauteous files.
He is they gracious friend
    And (O my soul awake!)
Did in pure love descend,
    To die here for thy sake.
If thou canst get but thither,
    There grows the flower of peace,
The rose that cannot wither,
    Thy fortress, and thy ease.
Leave then thy foolish ranges;
    For none can thee secure,
But one, who never changes,
    Thy God, thy life, thy cure.

Henry Vaughan

This England
(from *Richard II*)

This royal throne of kings, this sceptred isle,
This earth of majesty, this seat of Mars,
This other Eden, demi-paradise,
This fortress built by Nature for herself
Against infection and the hand of war,
This happy breed of men, this little world,
This precious stone set in the silver sea,
Which serves it in the office of a wall,
Or as a moat defensive to a house,
Against the envy of less happier lands,
This blessed plot, this earth, this realm, this England.

William Shakespeare

Jerusalem

And did those feet in ancient time
Walk upon England's mountains green?
And was the holy Lamb of God
On England's pleasant pastures seen?

And did the Countenance Divine
Shine forth upon our clouded hills?
And was Jerusalem builded here
Among these dark satanic mills?

Bring me my bow of burning gold!
Bring me my arrows of desire!
Bring me my spear! O clouds unfold!
Bring me my chariot of fire!

I will not cease from mental fight,
Nor shall my sword sleep in my hand
Till we have built Jerusalem
In England's green and pleasant land.

William Blake

Home thoughts from abroad

Oh, to be in England
Now that April's there,
And whoever wakes in England
Sees, some morning, unaware,
That the lowest boughs and the brushwood sheaf
Round the elm-tree bole are in tiny leaf,
While the chaffinch sings on the orchard bough
In England – now!
And after April, when May follows,
And the whitethroat builds, and all the swallows!
Hark, where my blossomed pear-tree in the hedge
Leans to the field and scatters on the clover
Blossoms and dewdrops – at the bent spray's edge –
That's the wise thrush; he sings each song twice over,
Lest you should think he never could recapture
The first fine careless rapture!
And though the fields look rough with hoary dew
All will be gay when noontide wakes anew
The buttercups, the little children's dower
– Far brighter than this gaudy melon-flower!

Robert Browning

15

The spring walk

We had a pleasant walk today,
Over the meadows and far away,
Across the bridge by the water-mill,
By the woodside, and up the hill;
And if you listen to what I say,
I'll tell you what we saw today:

We saw upon the shady banks,
   Long rows of golden flowers shine,
And first mistook for buttercups,
   The star-shaped yellow celandine.

Anemones and primroses,
   And the blue violets of spring,
We found while listening by a hedge
   To hear a merry ploughman sing.

And from the earth the plough turned up
   There came a sweet refreshing smell,
Such as the lily of the vale
   Sends forth from many a woodland dell.

We saw the yellow wallflower wave
   Upon a mouldering castle wall,
And then we watched the busy rooks
   Among the ancient elm-trees tall.

And leaning from the old stone bridge,
   Below we saw our shadows lie,
And though the gloomy arches watched
   The swift and fearless swallows fly.

Thomas Miller

A boy's song

Where the pools are bright and deep,
Where the grey trout lies asleep,
Up the river and over the lea,
That's the way for Billy and me.

Where the blackbird sings the latest,
Where the hawthorn blooms the sweetest,
Where the nestlings chirp and flee,
That's the way for Billy and me.

Where the mowers mow the cleanest,
Where the hay lies thick and greenest,
There to track the homeward bee,
That's the way for Billy and me.

Where the hazel bank is steepest,
Where the shadow falls the deepest,
Where the clustering nuts fall free,
That's the way for Billy and me.

Why the boys should drive away
Little sweet maidens from their play,
Or love to banter and fight so well,
That's the thing I never could tell.

But this I know, I love to play
Through the meadow, among the hay;
Up the water and over the lea,
That's the way for Billy and me.

James Hogg

Song

I wandered by the brook-side,
    I wandered by the mill,
I could not hear the brook flow,
    The noisy wheel was still;
There was no burr of grasshopper,
    No chirp of any bird;
But the beating of my own heart
    Was all the sound I heard.

I sat beneath the elm-tree,
    I watched the long, long shade,
And as it grew still longer
    I did not feel afraid;
For I listened for a footfall,
    I listened for a word –
But the beating of my own heart
    Was all the sound I heard.

He came not – no, he came not;
    The night came on alone;
The little stars sat one by one
    Each on his golden throne;
The evening air passed by my cheek,
    The leaves above were stirred –
But the beating of my own heart
    Was all the sound I heard.

Fast silent tears were flowing,
    When some one stood behind;
A hand was on my shoulder,
    I knew its touch was kind;
It drew me nearer – nearer;
    We did not speak a word –
For the beating of our own hearts
    Was all the sound we heard.

Richard Monckton Milnes

All day I hear the noise of waters

All day I hear the noise of waters
  Making moan,
Sad as the sea-bird is, when going
  Forth alone,
He hears the winds cry to the waters'
  Monotone.
The grey winds, the cold winds are blowing
  Where I go.
I hear the noise of many waters
  Far below.
All day, all night, I hear them flowing
  To and fro.

James Joyce

Piping down the valleys wild

Piping down the valleys wild,
Piping songs of pleasant glee,
On a cloud I saw a child,
And he laughing said to me:

'Pipe a song about a Lamb!'
So I piped with merry cheer.
'Piper, pipe that song again.'
So I piped: he wept to hear.

'Drop thy pipe, thy happy pipe,
Sing thy songs of happy cheer.'
So I sung the same again,
While he wept with joy to hear.

'Piper, sit thee down and write
In a book, that all may read.'
So he vanished from my sight,
And I plucked a hollow reed,

And I made a rural pen,
And I stained the water clear,
And I wrote my happy songs
Every child may joy to hear.

William Blake

I remember, I remember

I remember, I remember,
The house where I was born,
The little window where the sun
Came peeping in at morn;
He never came a wink too soon,
Nor brought too long a day,
But now, I often wish the night
Had borne my breath away!

I remember, I remember,
The roses, red and white,
The violets, and the lily-cups,
Those flowers made of light!
The lilacs where the robin built,
And where my brother set
The laburnum on his birthday –
The tree is living yet!

I remember, I remember,
Where I was used to swing,
And thought the air must rush as fresh
To swallows on the wing;
My spirit flew in feathers then,
That is so heavy now,
And summer pools could hardly cool
The fever on my brow!

I remember, I remember,
The fir trees dark and high;
I used to think their slender tops
Were close against the sky:
It was a childish ignorance,
But now 'tis little joy
To know I'm farther off from heaven
Than when I was a boy.

Thomas Hood

A child of our time

I remember, I remember
   The block where I was born,
The high-rise horror where the strain
   Left sleep and tempers torn.
Our flat was on the fourteenth floor,
   The shops were miles away,
And when the winter winds blew strong
   The whole thing seemed to sway.

I remember, I remember
   The lifts were on the blink,
And Mum would often say, 'This place
   Is driving me to drink.'
There was no room to swing a cat
   And little space to grow;
I longed for neighbours when I saw
   The human ants below.

I remember, I remember
   My father's worried frown,
The night the solid concrete cracked
   And most of it fell down.
I only hoped the architect
   Was living safe and sound,
The owner of a Georgian house
   And closer to the ground.

Roger Woddis

Why English is so hard

We'll begin with a box, and the plural is boxes;
But the plural of ox should be oxen, not oxes.
Then one fowl is goose, but two are called geese;
Yet the plural of moose should never be meese.
You may find a lone mouse or a whole lot of mice,
But the plural of house is houses, not hice.
If the plural of man is always called men,
Why shouldn't the plural of pan be called pen?
The cow in the plural may be cows or kine,
But the plural of vow is vows, not vine.
And I speak of a foot, and you show me your feet,
But I give you a boot – would a pair be called beet?
If one is a tooth and a whole set are teeth,
Why shouldn't the plural of booth be called beeth?
If the singular is this, and the plural is these,
Should the plural of kiss be nicknamed kese?
Then one may be that, and three may be those,
Yet the plural of hat would never be hose;
We speak of a brother, and also of brethren,
But though we say mother, we never say methren.
The masculine pronouns are he, his and him,
But imagine the feminine she, shis, and shim!
So our English, I think you will all agree,
Is the trickiest language you ever did see.

Unknown

25

Dunce

At school I never gained a prize,
Proving myself the model ass;
Yet how I watched with wistful eyes,
And cheered my mates who topped the class.
No envy in my heart I found,
Yet none was worthier to own
Those precious books in vellum bound,
Than I, a dreamer and a drone.

No prize at school I ever gained
(Shirking my studies, I suppose):
Yes, I remember being caned
For lack of love of Latin prose.
For algebra I won no praise,
In grammar I was far from bright:
Yet, oh, how Poetry would raise
In me a rapture of delight!

I never gained a prize at school;
The dullard's cap adorned my head;
My masters wrote me down a fool,
And yet – I'm sorry they are dead.
I'd like to go to them and say:
'Yours is indeed a tricky trade.
My honoured classmates, where are they?
Yet I, the dunce, brave books have made.'

Oh, I am old and worn and grey,
And maybe have not long to live;
Yet 'tis my hope at some Prize Day
At my old school the Head will give
A tome or two of mine to crown
Some pupil's well-deserved success –
Proving a scapegrace and a clown
May win at last to worthiness.

Robert Service

There was a little girl

There was a little girl,
And she had a little curl
  Right in the middle of her forehead.
When she was good
She was very, very good,
  And when she was bad she was horrid.

One day she went upstairs,
When her parents, unawares,
  In the kitchen were occupied with meals
And she stood upon her head
In her little trundle-bed,
  And then began hooraying with her heels.

Her mother heard the noise,
And she thought it was the boys
  A-playing at a combat in the attic;
But when she climbed the stair,
And found Jemima there,
  She took and she did spank her most emphatic.

Henry Wadsworth Longfellow

There was a naughty boy

There was a naughty boy,
    A naughty boy was he,
He would not stop at home,
    He could not quiet be –
        He took
        In his knapsack
        A book
        Full of vowels
        And a shirt
        With some towels –
        A slight cap
        For night cap –
        A hair brush,
        Comb ditto,
        New stockings
        For old ones
        Would split O!
        This knapsack
        Tight at's back
        He rivetted close
And followed his nose
    To the North,
    To the North,
And followed his nose
    To the North.

John Keats

Warning to children

Children, if you dare to think
Of the greatness, rareness, muchness,
Fewness of this precious only
Endless world in which you say
You live, you think of things like this:
Blocks of slate enclosing dappled
Red and green, enclosing tawny
Yellow nets, enclosing white
And black acres of dominoes,
Where a neat brown paper parcel
Tempts you to untie the string.
In the parcel a small island,
On the island a large tree,
On the tree a husky fruit.
Strip the husk and pare the rind off:
In the kernel you will see
Blocks of slate enclosed by dappled
Red and green, enclosed by tawny
Yellow nets, enclosed by white
And black acres of dominoes,
Where the same brown paper parcel –
Children, leave the string alone!
For who dares undo the parcel
Finds himself at once inside it,
On the island, in the fruit,
Blocks of slate about his head,
Finds himself enclosed by dappled
Green and red, enclosed by yellow
Tawny nets, enclosed by black
And white acres of dominoes,
With the same brown paper parcel
Still unopened on his knee.

And, if he then should dare to think
Of the fewness, muchness, rareness,
Greatness of this endless only
Precious world in which he says
He lives – he then unties the string.

Robert Graves

Young and old
(from *The Water Babies*)

When all the world is young, lad,
    And all the trees are green;
And every goose a swan, lad,
    And every lass a queen;
Then hey for boot and horse, lad,
    And round the world away;
Young blood must have its course, lad,
    And every dog his day.

When all the world is old, lad,
    And all the trees are brown;
And all the sport is stale, lad,
    And all the wheels run down;
Creep home, and take your place there,
    The spent and maimed among;
God grant you find one face there,
    You loved when all was young.

Charles Kingsley

If

If you can keep your head when all about you
    Are losing theirs and blaming it on you,
If you can trust yourself when all men doubt you,
    But make allowance for their doubting too;
If you can wait and not be tired by waiting,
    Or being lied about, don't deal in lies,
Or being hated don't give way to hating,
    And yet don't look too good, nor talk too wise:

If you can dream – and not make dreams your master;
    If you can think – and not make thoughts your aim:
If you can meet with Triumph and Disaster
    And treat those two impostors just the same;
If you can bear to hear the truth you've spoken
    Twisted by knaves to make a trap for fools,
Or watch the things you gave your life to, broken,
    And stoop and build 'em up with worn-out tools:

If you can make one heap of all your winnings
    And risk it on one turn of pitch-and-toss,
And lose, and start again at your beginnings
    And never breathe a word about your loss;
If you can force your heart and nerve and sinew
    To serve your turn long after they are gone,
And so hold on when there is nothing in you
    Except the Will which says to them: 'Hold on!'

If you can talk with crowds and keep your virtue,
  Or walk with Kings – nor lose the common touch,
If neither foes nor loving friends can hurt you,
  If all men count with you, but none too much;
If you can fill the unforgiving minute
  With sixty seconds' worth of distance run,
Yours is the Earth and everything that's in it,
  And – which is more – you'll be a Man, my son!

Rudyard Kipling

A man of words and not of deeds

A man of words and not of deeds
Is like a garden full of weeds;
And when the weeds begin to grow,
It's like a garden full of snow;
And when the snow begins to fall,
It's like a bird upon the wall;
And when the bird away does fly,
It's like an eagle in the sky;
And when the sky begins to roar,
It's like a lion at the door;
And when the door begins to crack,
It's like a stick across your back;
And when your back begins to smart,
It's like a pen-knife in your heart;
And when your heart begins to bleed,
You're dead, and dead, and dead, indeed.

Unknown

Uncle Albert

When I was almost eight years old
My Uncle Albert came to stay;
He wore a watch-chain made of gold
And sometimes he would let me play
With both the chain and gleaming watch,
And though at times I might be rough
He never seemed to bother much.
He smelled of shaving-soap and snuff.
To me he was a kind of God,
Immensely wise and strong and kind,
And so I thought it rather odd
When I came home from school to find
Two strangers, menacing and tall,
In the parlour, looking grim
As Albert – suddenly quite small –
Let them rudely hustle him
Out to where a black car stood.
Both Albert and his watch and chain
Disappeared that day for good.
My parents said he'd gone to Spain.

Vernon Scannell

What has happened to Lulu?

What has happened to Lulu, mother?
　　What has happened to Lu?
There's nothing in her bed but an old rag doll
　　And by its side a shoe.

Why is her window wide, mother,
　　The curtain flapping free,
And only a circle on the dusty shelf
　　Where her money-box used to be?

Why do you turn your head, mother,
　　And why do the tear-drops fall?
And why do you crumble that note on the fire
　　And say it is nothing at all?

I woke to voices late last night,
　　I heard an engine roar.
Why do you tell me the things I heard
　　Were a dream and nothing more?

I heard somebody cry, mother,
　　In anger or in pain,
But now I ask you why, mother,
　　You say it was a gust of rain.

Why do you wander about as though
　　You don't know what to do?
What has happened to Lulu, mother?
　　What has happened to Lu?

Charles Causley

The story of fidgety Philip

One evening Philip's father said,
'You twist and squirm and shake your head.
Come, let us see if you are able
To sit quite still for once at table.'
But not a word
Had Philip heard.
He giggled
And wiggled
And wriggled
And tottered
And teetered
And rocked in his chair.
Till his father cried, 'Philip!
Sit still – or beware!'

Caring nothing for disaster,
Backwards, forwards, always faster,
Philip rocked – until the chair
Slipped from under. Then and there
Philip grabbed the table cloth,
Spilling everything: the broth,
Bread and butter, all the dishes,
Goblets, gravy, meat and fishes,
Cauliflower, garden greens,
Spinach, parsnips, peas and beans,
Pastry, puddings white and brown . . .
Everything came tumbling down!

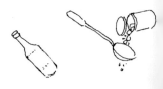

Meanwhile where was Philip? There,
Underneath the ruined chair,
Underneath – as you might guess –
Broken plates, a horrid mess,
Groaning in a hideous mood,
Soaked from head to toe with food.
And, to make his plight complete,
Nothing left for him to eat!

Heinrich Hoffman

Buckingham Palace

They're changing guard at Buckingham Palace –
Christoper Robin went down with Alice.
Alice is marrying one of the guard.
'A soldier's life is terrible hard,'
                                        Says Alice.

They're changing guard at Buckingham Palace –
Christopher Robin went down with Alice.
We saw a guard in a sentry-box.
'One of the sergeants looks after their socks,'
                                        Says Alice.

They're changing guard at Buckingham Palace –
Christopher Robin went down with Alice.
We looked for the King, but he never came.
'Well, God take care of him, all the same,'
                                        Says Alice.

They're changing guard at Buckingham Palace –
Christopher Robin went down with Alice.
They've great big parties inside the grounds.
'I wouldn't be King for a hundred pounds,'
                                        Says Alice.

They're changing guard at Buckingham Palace –
Christopher Robin went down with Alice.
A face looked out, but it wasn't the King's.
'He's much too busy a-signing things,'
                                        Says Alice.

They're changing guard at Buckingham Palace –
Christopher Robin went down with Alice.
'Do you think the King knows all about *me*?'
'Sure to, dear, but it's time for tea,'
                              Says Alice.

                              A. A. Milne

Matilda –
Who told lies, and was burned
to death

Matilda told such dreadful lies,
It made one gasp and stretch one's eyes;
Her Aunt, who, from her earliest youth,
Had kept a strict regard for truth,
Attempted to believe Matilda:
The effort very nearly killed her,
And would have done so, had not she
Discovered this infirmity.
For once, towards the close of day,
Matilda, growing tired of play,
And finding she was left alone,
Went tiptoe to the telephone
And summoned the immediate aid
Of London's noble fire-brigade.
Within an hour the gallant band
Were pouring in on every hand,
From Putney, Hackney Downs, and Bow
With courage high and hearts a-glow
They galloped, roaring through the town,
'Matilda's house is burning down!'

Inspired by British cheers and loud
Proceeding from the frenzied crowd,
They ran their ladders through a score
Of windows on the ballroom floor;
And took peculiar pains to souse
The pictures up and down the house,
Until Matilda's Aunt succeeded
In showing them they were not needed;
And even then she had to pay
To get the men to go away!

It happened that a few weeks later
Her Aunt was off to the theatre
To see that interesting play
The Second Mrs Tanqueray.
She had refused to take her niece
To hear this entertaining piece:
A deprivation just and wise
To punish her for telling lies.
That night a fire *did* break out –
You should have heard Matilda shout!
You should have heard her scream and bawl,
And throw the window up and call
To people passing in the street –
(The rapidly increasing heat
Encouraging her to obtain
Their confidence) – but all in vain!
For every time she shouted 'Fire!'
They only answered 'Little liar!'
And therefore when her Aunt returned,
Matilda, and the house, were burned.

Hilaire Belloc

40

Johnnie Crack and Flossie Snail
(from *Under Milk Wood*)

Johnnie Crack and Flossie Snail
Kept their baby in a milking pail
Flossie Snail and Johnnie Crack
One would pull it out and one would put
    it back.

O it's my turn now said Flossie Snail
To take the baby from the milking pail
And it's my turn now said Johnnie Crack
To smack it on the head and put it back.

Johnnie Crack and Flossie Snail
Kept their baby in a milking pail
One would put it back and one would pull
    it out
And all it had to drink was ale and stout
For Johnnie Crack and Flossie Snail
Always used to say that stout and ale
Was *good* for a baby in a milking pail.

Dylan Thomas

Hunter trials

It's awf'lly bad luck on Diana,
　　Her ponies have swallowed their bits;
She fished down their throats with a spanner
　　And frightened them all into fits.

So now she's attempting to borrow.
　　Do lend her some bits, Mummy, *do*;
I'll lend her my own for tomorrow,
　　But today *I*'ll be wanting them too.

Just look at Prunella on Guzzle,
　　The wizardest pony on earth;
Why doesn't she slacken his muzzle
　　And tighten the breech in his girth?

I say, Mummy, there's Mrs Geyser
　　And doesn't she look pretty sick?
I bet it's because Mona Lisa
　　Was hit on the hock with a brick.

Miss Blewitt says Monica threw it,
　　But Monica says it was Joan,
And Joan's very thick with Miss Blewitt,
　　So Monica's sulking alone.

And Margaret failed in her paces,
　　Her withers got tied in a noose,
So her coronets caught in the traces
　　And now all her fetlocks are loose.

Oh, it's me now. I'm terribly nervous.
　　I wonder if Smudges will shy.
She's practically certain to swerve as
　　Her Pelham is over one eye.

　　*　　*　　*　　*　　*

Oh wasn't it naughty of Smudges?
　　Oh, Mummy, I'm sick with disgust.
She threw me in front of the Judges,
　　And my silly old collarbone's bust.

John Betjeman

My sister Jane

And I say nothing – no, not a word
About our Jane. Haven't you heard?
She's a bird, a bird, a bird, a bird.
Oh it never would do to let folks know
My sister's nothing but a great big crow.

Each day (we daren't send her to school)
She pulls on stockings of thick blue wool
To make her pin crow legs look right,
Then fits a wig of curls on tight,
And dark spectacles – a huge pair
To cover her very crowy stare.
Oh it never would do to let folks know
My sister's nothing but a great big crow.

When visitors come she sits upright
(With her wings and her tail tucked out of sight).
They think her queer but extremely polite.
Then when the visitors have gone
She whips out her wings and with her wig on
Whirls through the house at the height of your head –
Duck, duck, or she'll knock you dead.
Oh it never would do to let folks know
My sister's nothing but a great big crow.

At meals whatever she sees she'll stab it –
Because she's a crow and that's a crow habit.
My mother says 'Jane! Your manners! Please!'
Then she'll sit quietly on the cheese,
Or play the piano nicely by dancing on the keys –
Oh it never would do to let folks know
My sister's nothing but a great big crow.

Ted Hughes

Two old crows

Two old crows sat on a fence rail.
Two old crows sat on a fence rail,
Thinking of effect and cause,
Of weeds and flowers,
And nature's laws.
One of them muttered, one of them stuttered,
One of them stuttered, one of them muttered.
Each of them thought far more than he uttered.
One crow asked the other crow a riddle.
One crow asked the other crow a riddle:
The muttering crow
Asked the stuttering crow,
'Why does a bee have a sword to his fiddle?
Why does a bee have a sword to his fiddle?'
'Bee-cause,' said the other crow,
'Bee-cause,
B B B B B B B B B B B B B B B B-Cause.'
Just then a bee flew close to their rail . . .
'Buzzzzzzzzzzzzzzzzzzzz   zzzzzzzzz   zzzzzzzzzzzzzzz
     ZZZZZZZZZ.'
And those two black crows
Turned pale,
And away those crows did sail.
Why?
B B B B B B B B B B B B B B B-cause.
B B B B B B B B B B B B B B B-cause.
'Buzzzzzzzzzzzzzzzzzzzz   zzzzzzzzz   zzzzzzzzzzzzzzz
     ZZZZZZZZZ.'

Vachel Lindsay

The raven

Underneath an old oak tree
There was of swine a huge company,
That grunted as they crunched the mast:
For that was ripe, and fell full fast.
Then they trotted away, for the wind grew high:
One acorn they left, and no more might you spy.
Next came a Raven, that liked not such folly:
He belonged, they did say, to the witch Melancholy!
Blacker was he than blackest jet,
Flew low in the rain, and his feather not wet.

He picked up the acorn and buried it straight
By the side of a river both deep and great.
      Where then did the Raven go?
      He went high and low,
Over hill, over dale, did the black Raven go.
      Many Autumns, many Springs
      Travelled he with wandering wings:
      Many Summers, many Winters –
      I can't tell half his adventures.

At length he came back, and with him a She,
And the acorn was grown to a tall oak tree.
They built them a nest in the topmost bough,
And young ones they had, and were happy enow.
But soon came a Woodman in leathern guise,
His brow, like a pent-house, hung over his eyes.
He'd an axe in his hand, not a word he spoke,
But with many a hem! and a sturdy stroke,
At length he brought down the poor Raven's own oak.
His young ones were killed; for they could not depart,
And their mother did die of a broken heart.

The boughs from the trunk the Woodman did sever;
And they floated it down on the course of the river.
They sawed it in planks, and its bark they did strip,
And with this tree and others they made a good ship.
The ship, it was launched; but in sight of the land
Such a storm there did rise as no ship could withstand.
It bulged on a rock, and the waves rushed in fast:
Round and round flew the Raven, and cawed to the
    blast.

He heard the last shriek of the perishing souls –
See! see! o'er the topmast the mad watèr rolls!
    Right glad was the Raven, and off he went
        fleet,
And Death riding home on a cloud he did meet,
And he thanked him again and again for this treat:
    They had taken his all, and revenge it was
        sweet!

Samuel Taylor Coleridge

47

The wreck of the Hesperus

It was the schooner Hesperus,
    That sailed the wintry sea;
And the skipper had taken his little daughter,
    To bear him company.

Blue were her eyes as the fairy flax,
    Her cheeks like the dawn of day,
And her bosom white as the hawthorn-buds,
    That open in the month of May.

The skipper he stood beside the helm,
    His pipe was in his mouth,
And he watched how the veering flaw did blow,
    The smoke now west, now south.

Then up and spake an old sailor,
    Had sailed the Spanish Main,
'I pray thee, put into yonder port,
    For I fear a hurricane.

'Last night, the moon had a golden ring,
    And tonight no moon we see!'
The skipper, he blew a whiff from his pipe,
    And a scornful laugh laughed he.

Colder and louder blew the wind,
    A gale from the north-east;
The snow fell hissing in the brine,
    And the billows frothed like yeast.

Down came the storm, and smote amain
    The vessel in its strength;
She shuddered and paused, like a frighted steed,
    Then leaped her cable's length.

'Come hither! come hither! my little daughter,
    And do not tremble so;
For I can weather the roughest gale,
    That ever wind did blow.'

He wrapped her warm in his seaman's coat,
    Against the stinging blast;
He cut a rope from a broken spar,
    And bound her to the mast.

'O father! I hear the church-bells ring,
    O say, what may it be?'
' 'Tis a fog-bell on a rock-bound coast!'
    And he steered for the open sea.

'O father! I hear the sound of guns,
    O say what may it be?'
'Some ship in distress, that cannot live
    In such an angry sea!'

'O father! I see a gleaming light,
    O say what may it be?'
But the father answered never a word,
    A frozen corpse was he.

Lashed to the helm, all stiff and stark,
    With his face turned to the skies,
The lantern gleamed through the gleaming snow
    On his fixed and glassy eyes.

Then the maiden clasped her hands and prayed
    That saved she might be;
And she thought of Christ who stilled the wave
    On the lake of Galilee.

And fast through the midnight dark and drear,
    Through the whistling sleet and snow,
Like a sheeted ghost, the vessel swept
    Towards the reef of Norman's Woe.

And ever the fitful gusts between
    A sound came from the land;
It was the sound of the trampling surf,
    On the rocks and the hard sea-sand.

The breakers were right beneath her bows,
    She drifted a dreary wreck,
And a whooping billow swept the crew
    Like icicles from her deck.

She struck where the white and fleecy waves
  Looked soft as carded wool,
But the cruel rocks they gored her side
  Like the horns of an angry bull.

Her rattling shrouds, all sheathed in ice,
  With the masts went by the board;
Like a vessel of glass, she stove and sank,
  Ho! ho! the breakers roared!

At day-break, on the bleak sea-beach,
  A fisherman stood aghast,
To see the form of a maiden fair,
  Lashed close to a drifting mast.

The salt sea was frozen on her breast,
  The salt tears in her eyes;
And he saw her hair, like the brown seaweed,
  On the billows fall and rise.

Such was the wreck of the Hesperus,
  In the midnight and the snow!
Christ save us all from a death like this,
  On the reef of Norman's Woe!

Henry Wadsworth Longfellow

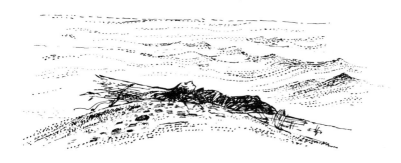

The Inchcape rock

No stir in the air, no stir in the sea –
The ship was as still as she could be;
Her sails from heaven received no motion;
Her keel was steady in the ocean.

Without either sign or sound of their shock,
The waves flowed over the Inchcape rock;
So little they rose, so little they fell,
They did not move the Inchcape bell.

The holy Abbot of Aberbrothok
Had placed that bell on the Inchcape rock;
On a buoy in the storm it floated and swung
And over the waves its warning rung.

When the rock was hid by the surges' swell,
The mariners heard the warning bell;
And then they knew the perilous rock,
And blessed the Abbot of Aberbrothok.

The sun in heaven was shining gay –
All things were joyful on that day;
The sea-birds screamed as they wheeled around,
And there was joyance in their sound.

The buoy of the Inchcape bell was seen,
A darker speck on the ocean green;
Sir Ralph, the rover, walked his deck,
And he fixed his eyes on the darker speck.

His eye was on the bell and float:
Quoth he, 'My men, put out the boat;
And row me to the Inchcape rock,
And I'll plague the priest of Aberbrothok.'

The beat is lowered, the boatmen row,
And to the Inchcape rock they go;
Sir Ralph bent over from the boat,
And cut the warning bell from the float.

Down sank the bell with a gurgling sound;
The bubbles rose, and burst around.
Quoth Sir Ralph, 'The next who comes to the rock
Will not bless the Abbot of Aberbrothok.'

Sir Ralph, the rover, sailed away –
He scoured the seas for many a day;
And now, grown rich with plundered store,
He steers his course to Scotland's shore.

So thick a haze o'erspreads the sky
They cannot see the sun on high;
The wind hath blown a gale all day;
At evening it hath died away.

On the deck the rover takes his stand;
So dark it is they see no land.
Quoth Sir Ralph, 'It will be lighter soon,
For there is the dawn of the rising moon.'

'Canst hear,' said one, 'the breakers roar?
For yonder, methinks, should be the shore.
Now where we are I cannot tell,
But I wish we could hear the Inchcape bell.'

They hear no sound; the swell is strong;
Though the wind hath fallen, they drift along;
Till the vessel strikes with a shivering shock –
O Christ! it is the Inchcape rock!

Sir Ralph, the rover, tore his hair;
He cursed himself in his despair.
The waves rush in on every side;
The ship is sinking beneath the tide.

But ever in his dying fear
One dreadful sound he seemed to hear –
A sound as if with the Inchcape bell
The Devil below was ringing his knell.

Robert Southey

Columbus

Behind him lay the gray Azores,
    Behind the Gates of Hercules;
Before him not the ghost of shores,
    Before him only shoreless seas.
The good mate said: 'Now must we pray,
    For lo! the very stars are gone.
Brave Admiral, speak, what shall I say?'
    'Why, say, "Sail on! sail on! and on!" '

'My men grow mutinous day by day;
    My men grow ghastly wan and weak.'
The stout mate thought of home: a spray
    Of salt wave washed his swarthy cheek.

'What shall I say, brave Admiral, say,
        If we sight naught but seas at dawn?'
'Why, you shall say at break of day,
        "Sail on! sail on! sail on! and on!" '

They sailed and sailed, as winds might blow,
        Until at last the blanched mate said:
'Why, now not even God would know
        Should I and all my men fall dead.
These very winds forget their way,
        For God from these dread seas is gone.
Now speak, brave Admiral, speak and say' –
        He said: 'Sail on! sail on! and on!'

They sailed. They sailed. Then spake the mate:
        'This mad sea shows his teeth tonight.
He curls his lip, he lies in wait,
        With lifted teeth as if to bite!
Brave Admiral, say but one good word:
        What shall we do when hope is gone?'
The words leapt like a leaping sword:
        'Sail on! sail on! sail on! and on!'

Then, pale and worn, he kept his deck,
        And peered through darkness. Ah, that night
Of all dark nights! And then a speck –
        A light! A light! A light! A light!
It grew, a starlit flag unfurled!
        It grew to be Time's burst of dawn.
He gained a world; he gave that world
        Its grandest lesson: 'On! sail on!'

Joaquin Miller

The Owl and the Pussy-Cat

The Owl and the Pussy-Cat went to sea
    In a beautiful pea-green boat,
They took some honey, and plenty of money,
    Wrapped up in a five-pound note.
The Owl looked up to the stars above,
    And sang to a small guitar,
'O lovely Pussy! O Pussy, my love,
    What a beautiful Pussy you are,
        You are,
        You are!
    What a beautiful Pussy you are!'

Pussy said to the Owl, 'You elegant fowl!
　　How charmingly sweet you sing!
O let us be married! too long we have tarried:
　　But what shall we do for a ring?'
They sailed away for a year and a day,
　　To the land where the Bong-tree grows,
And there in a wood a Piggy-wig stood,
　　With a ring at the end of his nose,
　　　His nose,
　　　His nose,
　　With a ring at the end of his nose.

'Dear Pig, are you willing to sell for one shilling
　　Your ring?' Said the Piggy, 'I will.'
So they took it away, and were married next day
　　By the Turkey who lives on the hill.
They dined on mince, and slices of quince,
　　Which they ate with a runcible spoon;
And hand in hand, on the edge of the sand,
　　They danced by the light of the moon,
　　　The moon,
　　　The moon,
　　They danced by the light of the moon.

Edward Lear

The sands of Dee

'O Mary, go and call the cattle home,
    And call the cattle home,
    And call the cattle home
  Across the sands of Dee';
The western wind was wild and dank with foam,
  And all alone went she.

The western tide crept up along the sand,
    And o'er and o'er the sand,
    And round and round the sand,
  As far as eye could see.
The rolling mist came down and hid the land:
  And never home came she.

'Oh! is it weed, or fish, or floating hair –
    A tress of golden hair,
    A drowned maiden's hair
  Above the nets at sea?
Was never salmon yet that shone so fair
  Among the stakes on Dee.'

They rowed her in across the rolling foam,
    The cruel crawling foam,
    The cruel hungry foam,
  To her grave beside the sea:
But still the boatmen hear her call the cattle home
  Across the sands of Dee.

Charles Kingsley

Little Billee

There were three sailors of Bristol city
Who took a boat and went to sea.
But first with beef and captain's biscuits
And pickled pork they loaded she.

There was gorging Jack and guzzling Jimmy,
And the youngest he was little Bill-ee.
Now when they got as far as the Equator
They'd nothing left but one split pea.

Says gorging Jack to guzzling Jimmy,
'I am extremely hungaree.'
To gorging Jack says guzzling Jimmy,
'We've nothing left, we must eat we.'

Says gorging Jack to guzzling Jimmy,
'With one another we shouldn't agree!
There's little Bill, he's young and tender,
We're old and tough, so let's eat he.

'Oh, Billy, we're going to kill and eat you,
So undo the button of your chemie.'
When Bill received this information
He used his pocket handkerchie.

'First let me say my catechism,
Which my poor mammy taught to me.'
'Make haste, make haste,' says guzzling Jimmy,
While Jack pulled out his snickersnee.

So Billy went up to the main-top gallant mast,
And down he fell on his bended knee.
He scarce had come to the twelfth commandment
When up he jumps. 'There's land I see:

'Jerusalem and Madagascar,
And North and South Amerikee:
There's the British flag a-riding at anchor,
With Admiral Napier, KCB.'

So when they got aboard of the Admiral's,
He hanged fat Jack and flogged Jimmee:
But as for little Bill he made him
The Captain of a Seventy-three.

William Makepeace Thackeray

The Golden Journey to Samarkand

We who with songs beguile your pilgrimage
    And swear that Beauty lives though lilies die,
We Poets of the proud old lineage
    Who sing to find your hearts, we know not why –

What shall we tell you? Tales, marvellous tales
    Of ships and stars and isles where good men rest,
Where nevermore the rose of sunset pales,
    And winds and shadows fall toward the West:

And there the world's first huge white-bearded kings
    In dim glades sleeping, murmur in their sleep,
And closer round their breasts the ivy clings,
    Cutting its pathway slow and red and deep.

And how beguile you? Death has no repose
    Warmer and deeper than that Orient sand
Which hides the beauty and bright faith of those
    Who made the Golden Journey to Samarkand.

And now they wait and whiten peaceably,
    Those conquerors, those poets, those so fair:
They know time comes, not only you and I,
    But the whole world shall whiten, here or there;

When those long caravans that cross the plain
    With dauntless feet and sound of silver bells
Put forth no more for glory or for gain,
    Take no more solace from the palm-girt wells.

When the great markets by the sea shut fast
    All that calm Sunday that goes on and on:
When even lovers find their peace at last,
    And Earth is but a star, that once had shone.

James Elroy Flecker

The Rubaiyat of Omar Khayyam
(a short extract)

Oh, come with old Khayyam and leave the Wise
To talk; one thing is certain, that Life flies;
    One thing is certain, and the Rest is Lies;
The Flower that once has blown for ever dies.

Myself when young did eagerly frequent
Doctor and Saint, and heard great Argument
    About it and about: but evermore
Came out by the same Door as in I went.

With them the Seed of Wisdom did I sow,
And with my own hand laboured it to grow:
    And this was all the Harvest that I reaped –
'I came like Water, and like Wind I go.'

Into this Universe, and *why* not knowing,
Nor *whence*, like Water willy-nilly flowing:
    And out of it, as Wind along the Waste,
I know not whither, willy-nilly blowing.

'Tis all a Chequer-board of Nights and Days
Where Destiny with Men for Pieces plays:
    Hither and thither moves, and mates, and slays,
And one by one back in the Closet lays.

The Ball no Question makes of Ayes and Noes.
But Right or Left, as strikes the Player goes;
    And he that tossed Thee down into the Field,
He knows about it all – He knows – He knows!

The Moving Finger writes; and having writ,
Moves on: nor all thy Piety nor Wit
    Shall lure it back to cancel half a Line,
Nor all thy Tears wash out a Word of it.

And that inverted Bowl we call The Sky,
Whereunder crawling cooped we live and die,
    Lift not thy hands to *It* for help – for It
Rolls impotently on as Thou or I.

Edward FitzGerald

Kubla Khan

In Xanadu did Kubla Khan
A stately pleasure-dome decree:
Where Alph, the sacred river, ran
Through caverns measureless to man
    Down to a sunless sea.
So twice five miles of fertile ground
With walls and towers were girdled round:
And here were gardens bright with sinuous rills
Where blossomed many an incense-bearing tree;
And here were forests ancient as the hills,
'Enfolding sunny spots of greenery.
But oh! that deep romantic chasm which slanted
Down the green hill athwart a cedarn cover!
A savage place! as holy and enchanted
As e'er beneath a waning moon was haunted
By woman wailing for her demon-lover!
And from this chasm, with ceaseless turmoil seething,
As if this earth in fast thick pants were breathing,
A mighty fountain momently was forced;
Amid whose swift half-intermitted burst
Huge fragments vaulted like rebounding hail,
Or chaffy grain beneath the thresher's flail:
And 'mid these dancing rocks at once and ever
It flung up momently the sacred river.
Five miles meandering with a mazy motion
Through wood and dale the sacred river ran,
Then reached the caverns measureless to man,
And sank in tumult to a lifeless ocean:
And 'mid this tumult Kubla heard from far
Ancestral voices prophesying war!

The shadow of the dome of pleasure
Floated midway on the waves;
Where was heard the mingled measure
From the fountain and the caves.
It was a miracle of rare device,
A sunny pleasure-dome with caves of ice!

A damsel with a dulcimer
In a vision once I saw:
It was an Abyssinian maid,
And on her dulcimer she played,
Singing of Mount Abora.
Could I revive within me
Her symphony and song,
To such a deep delight 'twould win me,
That with music loud and long,
I would build that dome in air,
That sunny dome! those caves of ice!
And all who heard should see them there,
And all should cry, Beware! Beware!
His flashing eyes, his floating hair!
Weave a circle round him thrice,
And close your eyes with holy dread,
For he on honey-dew hath fed,
And drunk the milk of Paradise.

Samuel Taylor Coleridge

The listeners

'Is there anybody there?' said the Traveller,
    Knocking on the moonlit door;
   And his horse in the silence champed the grasses
    Of the forest's ferny floor:
And a bird flew up out of the turret,
    Above the Traveller's head:
And he smote upon the door again a second time;
    'Is there anybody there?' he said.
But no one descended to the Traveller;
    No head from the leaf-fringed sill
Leaned over and looked into his grey eyes,
    Where he stood perplexed and still.
But only a host of phantom listeners
    That dwelt in the lone house then
Stood listening in the quiet of the moonlight
    To that voice from the world of men:
Stood thronging the faint moonbeams on the dark
    stair,
    That goes down to the empty hall,
Hearkening in an air stirred and shaken
    By the lonely Traveller's call.
And he felt in his heart their strangeness,
    Their stillness answering his cry,
While his horse moved, cropping the dark turf,
    'Neath the starred and leafy sky;
For he suddenly smote on the door, even
    Louder, and lifted his head:
'Tell them I came, and no one answered,
    That I kept my word,' he said.
Never the least stir made the listeners,
    Though every word he spake
Fell echoing through the shadowiness of the still
    house

From the one man left awake:
Ay, they heard his foot upon the stirrup,
  And the sound of iron on stone,
And how the silence surged softly backward,
  When the plunging hoofs were gone.

Walter de la Mare

Windy nights

Whenever the moon and stars are set,
   Whenever the wind is high,
All night long in the dark and wet,
   A man goes riding by.
Late in the night when the fires are out,
Why does he gallop and gallop about?

Whenever the trees are crying aloud,
   And ships are tossed at sea,
By, on the highway, low and loud,
   By at the gallop goes he.
By at the gallop he goes, and then
By he comes back at the gallop again.

Robert Louis Stevenson

The highwayman

PART ONE

The wind was a torrent of darkness among the gusty
    trees.
The moon was a ghostly galleon tossed upon cloudy
    seas.
The road was a ribbon of moonlight over the purple
    moor,
And the highwayman came riding—
       Riding—riding—
The highwayman came riding, up to the old inn-door.

He'd a French cocked-hat on his forehead, a bunch of
    lace at his chin,
A coat of the claret velvet, and breeches of brown
    doe-skin.
They fitted with never a wrinkle. His boots were up
    to the thigh.
And he rode with a jewelled twinkle,
       His pistol butts a-twinkle,
His rapier hilt a-twinkle, under the jewelled sky.

Over the cobbles he clattered and clashed in the dark
    inn-yard.
He tapped with his whip on the shutters, but all was
    locked and barred.
He whistled a tune to the window, and who should be
    waiting there
But the landlord's black-eyed daughter,
       Bess, the landlord's daughter,
Plaiting a dark red love-knot into her long black hair.

And dark in the dark old inn-yard a stable-wicket
    creaked
Where Tim the ostler listened. His face was white and
    peaked.
His eyes were hollows of madness, his hair like
    mouldy hay,
But he loved the landlord's daughter,
      The landlord's red-lipped daughter.
Dumb as a dog he listened, and he heard the robber
    say—

'One kiss, my bonny sweetheart, I'm after a prize
    tonight,
But I shall be back with the yellow gold before the
    morning light;
Yet, if they press me sharply, and harry me through
    the day,
Then look for me by moonlight,
      Watch for me by moonlight,
I'll come to thee by moonlight, though hell should bar
    the way.'

He rose upright in the stirrups. He scarce could reach
    her hand,
But she loosened her hair in the casement. His face
    burnt like a brand
As the black cascade of perfume came tumbling over
    his breast;
And he kissed its waves in the moonlight,
      (O, sweet black waves in the moonlight!)
Then he tugged at his rein in the moonlight, and
    galloped away to the west.

PART TWO

He did not come in the dawning. He did not come at
    noon;
And out of the tawny sunset, before the rise of the
    moon,
When the road was a gypsy's ribbon, looping the
    purple moor,
A red-coat troop came marching—
        Marching—marching—
King George's men came marching, up to the old inn-
    door.

They said no word to the landlord. They drank his ale
    instead.
But they gagged his daughter, and bound her, to the
    foot of her narrow bed.
Two of them knelt at her casement, with muskets at
    their side!
There was death at every window;
        And hell at one dark window;
For Bess could see, through her casement, the road
    that *he* would ride.

They had tied her up to attention, with many a
    sniggering jest.
They had bound a musket beside her, with the muzzle
    beneath her breast!
'Now, keep good watch!' and they kissed her. She
    heard the doomed man say—
Look for me by moonlight;
        Watch for me by moonlight;
I'll come to thee by moonlight, though hell should bar
    the way!

71

She twisted her hands behind her; but all the knots
    held good!
She writhed her hands till her fingers were wet with
    sweat or blood!
They stretched and strained in the darkness, and the
    hours crawled by like years,
Till, now, on the stroke of midnight,
       Cold, on the stroke of midnight,
The tip of one finger touched it! The trigger at least
    was hers!

The tip of one finger touched it. She strove no more
    for the rest.
Up, she stood up to attention, with the muzzle
    beneath her breast.
She would not risk their hearing; she would not strive
    again;
For the road lay bare in the moonlight;
       Blank and bare in the moonlight;
And the blood in her veins, in the moonlight,
    throbbed to her love's refrain.

Tlot-tlot; tlot-tlot! Had they heard it? The horsehoofs
    ringing clear;
Tlot-tlot, tlot-tlot, in the distance? Were they deaf that
    they did not hear?
Down the ribbon of moonlight, over the brow of the
    hill,
The highwayman came riding—
       Riding—riding—
The red-coats looked to their priming! She stood up,
    straight and still.

Tlot-tlot, in the frosty silence! *Tlot-tlot*, in the
    echoing night!
Nearer he came and nearer. Her face was like a light.
Her eyes grew wide for a moment; she drew one last
    deep breath,
Then her finger moved in the moonlight,
      Her musket shattered the moonlight,
Shattered her breast in the moonlight and warned
    him—with her death.

He turned. He spurred to the west; he did not know
    who stood
Bowed, with her head o'er the musket, drenched with
    her own blood!
Not till the dawn he heard it, and his face grew grey to
    hear
How Bess, the landlord's daughter,
      The landlord's black-eyed daughter,
Had watched for her love in the moonlight, and died
    in the darkness there.

Back, he spurred like a madman, shouting a curse to
    the sky,
With the white road smoking behind him and his
    rapier brandished high.
Blood-red were his spurs in the golden noon; wine-
    red was his velvet coat;
When they shot him down on the highway,
    Down like a dog on the highway,
And he lay in his blood on the highway, with a bunch
    of lace at his throat.

    *   *   *   *   *   *   *   *   *

*And still of a winter's night, they say, when the wind is
    in the trees,
When the moon is a ghostly galleon tossed upon cloudy
    seas,
When the road is a ribbon of moonlight over the purple
    moor,
A highwayman comes riding—
    Riding—riding—
A highwayman comes riding, up to the old inn-door.*

*Over the cobbles he clatters and clangs in the dark inn-
    yard.
He taps with his whip on the shutters, but all is locked
    and barred.
He whistles a tune to the window, and who should be
    waiting there
But the landlord's black-eyed daughter,
    Bess, the landlord's daughter,
Plaiting a dark red love-knot into her long black hair.*

Alfred Noyes

Winter the Huntsman

Through his iron glades
Rides Winter the Huntsman.
All colour fades
As his horn is heard sighing.

Far through the forest
His wild hooves crash and thunder
Till many a mighty branch
Is torn asunder.

And the red reynard creeps
To his hole near the river,
The copper leaves fall
And the bare trees shiver.

As night creeps from the ground,
Hides each tree from its brother,
And each dying sound
Reveals yet another.

Is it Winter the Huntsman
Who gallops through his iron glades,
Cracking his cruel whip
To the gathering shades?

Osbert Sitwell

How they brought the good news from Ghent to Aix

I sprang to the stirrup, and Joris, and he;
I galloped, Dirck galloped, we galloped all three;
'Good speed!' cried the watch, as the gate-bolts
    undrew;
'Speed!' echoed the wall to us galloping through;
Behind shut the postern, the lights sank to rest,
And into the midnight we galloped abreast.

Not a word to each other; we kept the great pace
Neck by neck, stride by stride, never changing our
    place;
I turned in my saddle and made its girths tight,
Then shortened each stirrup, and set the pique right,
Rebuckled the cheek-strap, chained slacker the bit,
Nor galloped less steadily Roland a whit.

'Twas moonset at starting; but while we drew near
Lokeren, the cocks crew and twilight dawned clear;
At Boom, a great yellow star came out to see;
At Duffeld, 'twas morning as plain as could be;
And from Mecheln church-steeple we heard the half-
    chime,
So Joris broke silence with, 'Yet there is time!'

At Aershot, up leaped of a sudden the sun
And against him the cattle stood black every one,
To stare thro' the mist at us galloping past,
And I saw my stout galloper Roland at last,
With resolute shoulders, each butting away
The haze, as some bluff river headland its spray,

And his low head and crest, just one sharp ear bent
    back
For my voice, and the other pricked out on his track;
And one eye's black intelligence – ever that glance
O'er its white edge at me, his own master, askance!
And the thick heavy spume-flakes which aye and anon
His fierce lips shook upwards in galloping on.

By Hasselt, Dirck groaned; and cried Joris, 'Stay
    spur!
Your Roos galloped bravely, the fault's not in her,
We'll remember at Aix' – for one heard the quick
    wheeze
Of her chest, saw the stretched neck and staggering
    knees,
And sunk tail, and horrible heave of the flank,
As down on her haunches she shuddered and sank.

So we were left galloping, Joris and I,
Past Looz and past Tongres, no cloud in the sky!
The broad sun above laughed a pitiless laugh,
'Neath our feet broke the brittle bright stubble like
    chaff;
Till over by Dalhem a dome-spire sprang white,
And 'Gallop', gasped Joris, 'for Aix is in sight!'

'How they'll greet us!' and all in a moment his roan
Rolled neck and croup over, lay dead as a stone;
And there was my Roland to bear the whole weight
Of the news which alone could save Aix from her fte,
With his nostrils like pits full of blood to the brim,
And with circles of red for his eye-sockets' rim.

Then I cast loose my buffcoat, each holster let fall,
Shook off both my jack-boots, let go belt and all,
Stood up in the stirrup, leaned, patted his ear,
Called my Roland his pet-name, my horse without
    peer;
Clapped my hands, laughed and sang, any noise bad
    or good,
Till at length into Aix Roland galloped and stood.

And all I remember is, friends flocking round
As I sat with his head 'twixt my knees on the ground,
And no voice but was praising this Roland of mine,
As I poured down his throat our last measure of wine,
Which (the burgesses voted by common consent)
Was no more than his due who brought good news
    from Ghent.

Robert Browning

The charge of the light brigade

Half a league, half a league,
Half a league onward,
All in the valley of Death
    Rode the six hundred.
'Forward, the Light Brigade!
Charge for the guns!' he said:
Into the valley of Death
    Rode the six hundred.

'Forward, the Light Brigade!'
Was there a man dismayed?
Not though the soldier knew
    Someone had blundered:
Theirs not to make reply,
Theirs not to reason why,
Theirs but to do and die:
Into the valley of Death
    Rode the six hundred.

Cannon to right of them,
Cannon to left of them,
Cannon in front of them
    Volley'd and thundered;
Stormed at with shot and shell,
Boldly they rode and well,
Into the jaws of Death,
Into the mouth of Hell
    Rode the six hundred.

Flashed all their sabres bare,
Flashed as they turned in air,
Sabring the gunners there,
Charging an army, while
    All the world wondered:
Plunged in the battery-smoke
Right through the line they broke;
Cossack and Russian
Reeled from the sabre-stroke
    Shattered and sundered.
Then they rode back, but not,
    Not the six hundred.

Cannon to the right of them,
Cannon to the left of them,
Cannon behind them
    Volley'd and thundered;
Stormed at with shot and shell,
While horse and hero fell,
They that had fought so well
Came through the jaws of Death
Back from the mouth of Hell,
All that was left of them,
    Left of the six hundred.

When can their glory fade?
O the wild charge they made!
    All the world wondered.
Honour the charge they made!
Honour the Light Brigade,
    Noble six hundred!

Alfred, Lord Tennyson

Hannibal

Hannibal crossed the Alps,
Hannibal crossed the Alps;
    With his black men,
    His brown men,
    His countrymen,
    His townmen,
With his Gauls and his Spaniards, his horses and
    elephants,
Hannibal crossed the Alps.

Hannibal crossed the Alps,
Hannibal crossed the Alps;
    For his bow-men,
    His spear-men,
    His front-men,
    His rear-men,
His Gauls and his Spaniards, his horses and elephants,
Wanted the Roman scalps!

And that's why
Hannibal, Hannibal, Hannibal,
Hannibal crossed the Alps.

Eleanor Farjeon

81

We'll go no more a-roving

So, we'll go no more a-roving
    So late into the night,
Though the heart be still as loving,
    And the moon be still as bright.

For the sword outwears its sheath,
    And the soul wears out the breast,
And the heart must pause to breathe,
    And love itself have rest.

Though the night was made for loving,
    And the day returns too soon,
Yet we'll go no more a-roving
    By the light of the moon.

Lord Byron

Silver

Slowly, silently, now the moon
Walks the night in her silver shoon;
This way, and that, she peers, and sees
Silver fruit upon silver trees;
One by one the casements catch
Her beams beneath the silvery thatch;
Couched in his kennel, like a log,
With paws of silver sleeps the dog;
From their shadowy cote the white breasts peep
Of doves in a silver-feathered sleep;
A harvest mouse goes scampering by,
With silver claws, and silver eye;
And moveless fish in the water gleam,
By silver reeds in a silver stream.

Walter de la Mare

The Lady of Shalott
(a short extract)

There she weaves by night and day
A magic web with colours gay.
She has heard a whisper say,
A curse is on her if she stay
        To look down to Camelot.
She knows not what the curse may be,
And so she weaveth steadily,
And little other care hath she,
        The Lady of Shalott.

And moving through a mirror clear
That hangs before her all the year,
Shadows of the world appear.
There she sees the highway near
        Winding down to Camelot:
There the river eddy whirls,
And there the surly village-churls,
And the red cloaks of market girls,
        Pass onward from Shalott.

Sometimes a troop of damsels glad,
An abbot on an ambling pad,
Sometimes a curly shepherd-lad,
Or long-haired page in crimson clad,
      Goes by to towered Camelot;
And sometimes through the mirror blue
The knights come riding two and two:
She hath no loyal knight and true,
      The Lady of Shalott.

But in her web she still delights
To weave the mirror's magic sights,
For often through the silent nights
A funeral, with plumes and lights,
      And music, went to Camelot:
Or when the moon was overhead,
Came two young lovers lately wed;
'I am half sick of shadows,' said
      The Lady of Shalott.

Alfred, Lord Tennyson

85

She walks in beauty

She walks in beauty, like the night
    Of cloudless climes and starry skies;
And all that's best of dark and bright
    Meet in her aspect and her eyes:
Thus mellowed to that tender light
    Which heaven to gaudy day denies.

One shade the more, one ray the less,
    Had half impaired the nameless grace
Which waves in every raven tress,
    Or softly lightens o'er her face;
Where thoughts serenely sweet express
    How pure, how dear their dwelling-place.

And on that cheek, and o'er that brow,
    So soft, so calm, yet eloquent,
The smiles that win, the tints that glow,
    But tell of days in goodness spent,
A mind at peace with all below,
    A heart whose love is innocent!

Lord Byron

A red, red rose

My love is like a red, red rose
    That's newly sprung in June:
My love is like the melody
    That's sweetly played in tune.

As fair art thou, my bonnie lass,
    So deep in love am I:
And I will love thee still, my dear,
    Till a' the seas gang dry.

Till a' the sea gang dry, my dear,
    And the rocks melt wi' the sun:
And I will love thee still, my dear,
    While the sands o' life shall run.

And fare thee weel, my only love,
    And fare thee weel a while!
And I will come again, my love,
    Thou' it were ten thousand mile.

Robert Burns

Mr Nobody

I know a funny little man,
    As quiet as a mouse,
Who does the mischief that is done
    In everybody's house!
There's no one ever sees his face,
    And yet we all agree
That every plate we break was cracked
    By Mr Nobody.

'Tis he who always tears our books,
    Who leaves the door ajar,
He pulls the buttons from our shirts,
    And scatters pins afar;
That squeaking door will always squeak,
    For prithee, don't you see,
We leave the oiling to be done
    By Mr Nobody.

He puts damp wood upon the fire,
    That kettles cannot boil;
His are the feet that bring in mud,
    And all the carpets soil.
The papers always are mislaid,
    Who had them last but he?
There's no one tosses them about
    But Mr Nobody.

The finger-marks upon the door
    By none of us are made;
We never leave the blinds unclosed,
    To let the curtains fade.
The ink we never spill; the boots
    That lying round you see
Are not our boots – they all belong
    To Mr Nobody.

Unknown

The talented man
(A letter from a lady in London to a lady in Lausanne)

Dear Alice, you'll laugh when you know it –
    Last week, at the Duchess's ball,
I danced with the clever new poet,
    You've heard of him – Tully St Paul.
Miss Jonquil was perfectly frantic;
    I wish you had seen Lady Anne!
It really was very romantic;
    He *is* such a talented man!

He came up from Brazennose College,
      'Just caught', as they call it, last Spring;
And his head, love, is stuffed full of knowledge
      Of every conceivable thing:
Of science and logic he chatters,
      As fine and as fast as he can;
Though *I* am no judge of such matters,
      I'm sure he's a talented man.

His stories and jests are delightful;
      Not stories or jests, dear, for *you* –
The jests are exceedingly spiteful,
      The stories not always *quite* true.
Perhaps to be kind and veracious
      May do pretty well at Lausanne;
But it never would answer – good gracious!
      Chez nous, in a talented man.

He sneers – how my Alice would scold him! –
      At the bliss of a sigh or a tear:
He laughed – only think – when I told him
      How we cried o'er Trevelyan last year.
I vow I was quite in a passion;
      I broke all the sticks of my fan;
But sentiment's quite out of fashion,
      It seems, in a talented man.

Lady Bab, who is terribly moral,
    Declared that poor Tully is vain,
And apt – which is silly – to quarrel,
    And fond – which is wrong – of champagne.
I listened and doubted, dear Alice;
    For I saw, when my Lady began,
It was only the Dowager's malice;
    She *does* hate a talented man!

He's hideous – I own it. But fame, love,
    Is all that these eyes can adore:
He's lame – but Lord Byron was lame, love;
    And dumpy – but so is Tom Moore.
Then his voice – *such* a voice! my sweet creature,
    It's like your Aunt Lucy's toucan;
But oh! what's a tone or a feature,
    When once one's a talented man?

My mother, you know, all the season,
    Has talked of Sir Geoffrey's estate;
And truly, to do the fool reason,
    He *has* been less horrid of late.
But today, when we drive in the carriage,
    I'll tell her to lay down her plan –
If ever I venture on marriage,
    It *must* be a talented man!

DORA

P.S. – I have found, on reflection,
    One fault in my friend – *entre nous*;
Without it he'd just be perfection;
    Poor fellow – he has not a *sou*.
And so, when he comes in September
    To shoot with my Uncle, Sir Dan,
I've promised Mamma to remember
    He's *only* a talented man!

Winthrop Mackworth Praed

Shadwell Stair

I am the ghost of Shadwell Stair.
  Along the wharves by the water-house,
  And through the dripping slaughter-house,
I am the shadow that walks there.

Yet I have flesh both firm and cool,
  And eyes tumultuous as the gems
  Of moons and lamps in the lapping Thames
When dusk sails wavering down the pool.

Shuddering the purple street-arc burns
  Where I watch always; from the banks
  Dolorously the shipping clanks,
And after me a strange tide turns.

I walk till the stars of London wane
  And dawn creeps up the Shadwell Stair.
  But when the crowning syrens blare
I with another ghost am lain.

Wilfred Owen

93

The night mail

This is the night mail crossing the border,
Bringing the cheque and the postal order,
Letters for the rich, letters for the poor,
The shop at the corner and the girl next door,
Pulling up Beattock, a steady climb –
The gradient's against her but she's on time.

Past cotton grass and moorland boulder,
Shovelling white steam over her shoulder,
Snorting noisily as she passes
Silent miles of wind-bent grasses;
Birds turn their heads as she approaches,
Stare from the bushes at her blank-faced coaches;
Sheepdogs cannot turn her course,
They slumber on with paws across;
In the farm she passes no one wakes
But a jug in a bedroom gently shakes.

Dawn freshens, the climb is done.
Down towards Glasgow she descends
Towards the steam tugs, yelping down the glade of
        cranes
Towards the fields of apparatus, the furnaces
Set on the dark plain like gigantic chessmen.
All Scotland waits for her;
In the dark glens, beside the pale-green sea lochs,
Men long for news.

Letters of thanks, letters from banks,
Letters of joy from the girl and boy,
Receipted bills and invitations
To inspect new stock or visit relations,
And applications for situations,
And timid lovers' declarations,
And gossip, gossip from all the nations,
News circumstantial, news financial,
Letters with holiday snaps to enlarge in,
Letters with faces scrawled on the margin.
Letters from uncles, cousins and aunts,
Letters to Scotland from the South of France,
Letters of condolence to Highlands and Lowlands,
Notes from overseas to the Hebrides;
Written on paper of every hue,
The pink, the violet, the white and the blue,
The chatty, the catty, the boring, adoring,
The cold and official and the heart's outpouring,
Clever, stupid, short and long,
The typed and the printed and the spelt all wrong.

Thousands are still asleep
Dreaming of terrifying monsters
Or a friendly tea beside the band at Cranston's or
        Crawford's;
Asleep in working Glasgow, asleep in well-set
        Edinburgh,
Asleep in granite Aberdeen.
They continue their dreams
But shall wake soon and long for letters.
And none will hear the postman's knock
Without a quckening of the heart,
For who can bear to feel himself forgotten?

                              W. H. Auden

Glass falling

The glass is going down. The sun
Is going down. The forecasts say
It will be warm, with frequent showers.
We ramble down the showery hours
And amble up and down the day.
Mary will wear her black goloshes
And splash the puddles on the town;
And soon on fleets of macintoshes
The rain is coming down, the frown
Is coming down of heaven showing
A wet night coming, the glass is going
Down, the sun is going down.

Louis MacNeice

Evening
(an extract)

The sun is set; the swallows are asleep;
    The bats are flitting fast in the grey air;
The slow soft toads out of dim corners creep,
    And evening's breath, wandering here and there
Over the quivering surface of the stream,
Wakes not one ripple from its summer dream.

There is no dew on the dry grass tonight,
    Nor damp within the shadow of the trees;
The wind is intermitting, dry, and light;
    And in the inconstant motion of the breeze
The dust and straws are driven up and down,
And whirled about the pavement of the town.

Percy Bysshe Shelley

The song of the Jellicles

Jellicle Cats come out tonight
Jellicle Cats come one come all:
The Jellicle Moon is shining bright –
Jellicles come to the Jellicle Ball.

Jellicle Cats are black and white,
Jellicle Cats are rather small;
Jellicle Cats are merry and bright,
And pleasant to hear when they caterwaul.
Jellicle Cats have cheerful faces,
Jellicle Cats have bright black eyes;
They like to practise their airs and graces
And wait for the Jellicle Moon to rise.

Jellicle Cats develop slowly,
Jellicle Cats are not too big;
Jellicle Cats are roly-poly,
They know how to dance a gavotte and a jig.
Until the Jellicle Moon appears
They make their toilette and take their repose:
Jellicles wash behind their ears,
Jellicles dry between their toes.

Jellicle Cats are white and black,
Jellicle Cats are of moderate size;
Jellicles jump like a jumping-jack,
Jellicle Cats have moonlit eyes.
They're quiet enough in the morning hours,
They're quiet enough in the afternoon,
Reserving their terpischorean powers
To dance by the light of the Jellicle Moon.

Jellicle Cats are black and white,
Jellicle Cats (as I said) are small;
If it happens to be a stormy night
They will practise a caper or two in the hall.
If it happens the sun is shining bright
You would say they had nothing to do at all:
They are resting and saving themselves to be right
For the Jellicle Moon and the Jellicle Ball.

T. S. Eliot

Midnight

Midnight was come, when every vital thing
With sweet sound sleep their weary limbs did rest,
The beasts were still, the little birds that sing
Now sweetly slept beside their mother's breast,
The old and all were shrouded in their nest;
The waters calm, the cruel seas did cease,
The woods, and fields, and all things held their peace.

The golden stars were whirled amid their race,
And on the earth did laugh with twinkling light,
When each thing, nestled in his resting place,
Forgot day's pain with pleasure of the night:
The hare had not the greedy hounds in sight,
The fearful deer of death stood not in doubt,
The partridge dreamed not of the falcon's foot.

The ugly bear now minded not the stake,
Nor how the cruel mastiffs do him tear;
The stag lay still unroused from the brake;
The foamy boar feared not the hunter's spear;
All things were still, in desert, bush, and brere:
With quiet heart, now from their travails ceased,
Soundly they slept in midst of all their rest.

Thomas Sackville

What is pink?

What is pink? a rose is pink
By the fountain's brink.
What is red? a poppy's red
In its barley bed.
What is blue? the sky is blue
Where the clouds float through.
What is white? a swan is white
Sailing in the light.
What is yellow? pears are yellow,
Rich and ripe and mellow.
What is green? the grass is green,
With small flowers between.
What is violet? clouds are violet
In the summer twilight.
What is orange? why, an orange,
Just an orange!

Christina Rossetti

The garden year

January brings the snow,
Makes our feet and fingers glow.

February brings the rain,
Thaws the frozen lake again.

March brings breezes, loud and shrill,
To stir the dancing daffodil.

April brings the primrose sweet,
Scatters daisies at our feet.

May brings flocks of pretty lambs
Skipping by their fleecy dams.

June brings tulips, lilies, roses,
Fills the children's hands with posies.

Hot July brings cooling showers,
Apricots, and gillyflowers.

August brings the sheaves of corn,
Then the harvest home is borne.

Warm September brings the fruit;
Sportsmen then begin to shoot.

Fresh October brings the pheasant;
Then to gather nuts is pleasant.

Dull November brings the blast;
Then the leaves are whirling fast.

Chill December brings the sleet,
Blazing fire, and Christmas treat.

Sara Coleridge

Triads

1

The word of the sun to the sky,
    The word of the wind to the sea,
        The word of the moon to the night,
            What may it be?

2

The sense to the flower of the fly,
    The sense of the bird to the tree,
        The sense to the cloud of the light,
            Who can tell me?

3

The song of the fields to the kye,
    The song of the lime to the bee,
        The song of the depth to the height,
            Who knows all three?

Algernon Charles Swinburne

Christmas

The bells of waiting Advent ring,
    The Tortoise stove is lit again
And lamp-oil light across the night
    Has caught the streaks of winter rain
In many a stained-glass window sheen
From Crimson Lake to Hooker's Green.

The holly in the windy hedge
    And round the Manor House the yew
Will soon be stripped to deck the ledge,
    The altar, font and arch and pew,
So that the villagers can say
'The church looks nice' on Christmas Day.

Provincial public houses blaze
    And Corporation tramcars clang,
On lighted tenements I gaze
    Where paper decorations hang,
And bunting in the red Town Hall
Says 'Merry Christmas to you all.'

And London shops on Christmas Eve
    Are strung with silver bells and flowers
As hurrying clerks the City leave
    To pigeon-haunted classic towers,
And marbled clouds go scudding by
The many-steepled London sky.

And girls in slacks remember Dad,
  And oafish louts remember Mum,
And sleepless children's hearts are glad,
  And Christmas-morning bells say 'Come!'
Even to shining ones who dwell
Safe in the Dorchester Hotel.

And is it true? And is it true,
  This most tremendous tale of all,
Seen in a stained-glass window's hue,
  A Baby in an ox's stall?
The Maker of the stars and sea
Become a Child on earth for me?

And is it true? For if it is,
  No loving fingers tying strings
Around those tissued fripperies,
  The sweet and silly Christmas things,
Bath salts and inexpensive scent
And hideous tie so kindly meant.

No love that in a family dwells,
  No carolling in frosty air,
Nor all the steeple-shaking bells
  Can with this single Truth compare –
That God was Man in Palestine
And lives today in Bread and Wine.

John Betjeman

Ring out, wild bells

Ring out, wild bells, to the wild sky,
    The flying cloud, the frosty light:
    The year is dying in the night;
Ring out, wild bells, and let him die.

Ring out the old, ring in the new,
    Ring, happy bells, across the snow:
    The year is going, let him go;
Ring out the false, ring in the true.

Ring out the grief that saps the mind,
    For those that here we see no more;
    Ring out the feud of rich and poor,
Ring in redress to all mankind.

Ring out a slowly dying cause,
    And ancient forms of party strife;
    Ring in the nobler modes of life,
With sweeter manners, purer laws.

Ring out the want, the care, the sin,
    The faithless coldness of the times;
    Ring out, ring out my mournful rhymes,
But ring the fuller minstrel in.

Ring out false pride in place and blood,
    The civic slander and the spite;
    Ring in the love of truth and right,
Ring in the common love of good.

Ring out old shapes of foul disease;
    Ring out the narrowing lust of gold;
    Ring out the thousand wars of old,
Ring in the thousand years of peace.

Ring in the valiant man and free,
    The larger heart, the kindlier hand;
    Ring out the darkness of the land,
Ring in the Christ that is to be.

Alfred, Lord Tennyson

London snow

When men were all asleep the snow came flying,
In large white flakes falling on the city brown,
Stealthily and perpetually settling and loosely lying,
    Hushing the latest traffic of the drowsy town;
Deadening, muffling, stifling its murmurs failing;
Lazily and incessantly floating down and down:
    Silently sifting and veiling road, roof and railing;
Hiding difference, making unevenness even,
Into angles and crevices softly drifting and sailing.
    All night it fell, and when full inches seven
It lay in the depth of its uncompacted lightness,
The clouds blew off from a high and frosty heaven;
    And all woke earlier for the unaccustomed
        brightness
Of the winter dawning, the strange unheavenly glare:
The eye marvelled – marvelled at the dazzling
        whiteness;
    The ear hearkened to the stillness of the solemn
        air;
No sound of wheel rumbling nor of foot falling,
And the busy morning cries came thin and spare.

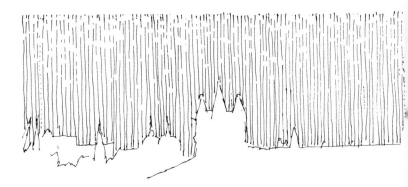

Then boys I heard, as they went to school,
        calling,
They gathered up the crystal manna to freeze
Their tongues with tasting, their hands with
        snowballing;
    Or rioted in a drift, plunging up to the knees;
Or peering up from under the white-mossed wonder,
'O look at the trees!' they cried, 'O look at the trees!'
    With lessened load a few carts creak and blunder,
Following along the white deserted way,
A country company long dispersed asunder:
    When now already the sun, in pale display
Standing by Paul's high dome, spread forth below
His sparkling beams, and awoke the stir of day.
    For now doors open, and war is waged with the
        snow;
And trains of sombre men, past tale of number,
Tread long brown paths, as toward their toil they go:
    But even for them awhile no cares encumber
Their minds diverted; the daily word is unspoken,
The daily thoughts of labour and sorrow slumber
At the sight of the beauty that greets them, for the
    charm they have broken.

Robert Bridges

A new year's burden

Along the grass sweet airs are blown
    Our way this day in Spring.
Of all the songs that we have known
    Now which one shall we sing?
        Not that, my love, ah no! –
        Not this, my love? why, so! –
Yet both were ours, but hours will come and go.

The grove is all a pale frail mist,
    The new year sucks the sun.
Of all the kisses that we kissed
    Now which shall be the one?
        Not that, my love, ah no! –
        Not this, my love? – heigh-ho
For all the sweets that all the winds can blow!

The branches cross above our eyes,
    The skies are in a net:
And what's the thing beneath the skies
    We two would most forget?
        Not birth, my love, no, no –
        Not death, my love, no, no –
The love once ours, but ours long hours ago.

Dante Gabriel Rossetti

The trees are bare
(from *The bluebell*)

The trees are bare, the sun is cold,
    And seldom, seldom seen;
The heavens have lost their zone of gold,
    And earth her robe of green.

And ice upon the glancing stream
    Has cast its sombre shade;
The distant hills and valleys seem
    In frozen mist arrayed.

And, oh! when chill the sunbeams fall
    Adown that dreary sky,
And gild yon dank and darkened wall
    With transient brilliancy.

How do I weep, how do I pine
    For the time of flowers to come,
And turn me from that fading shrine,
    To mourn the fields of home!

Emily Brontë

First primrose

I saw it in the lane
One morning going to school
After a soaking night of rain,
The year's first primrose,
Lying there familiar and cool
In its private place
Where little else grows
Beneath dripping hedgerows,
Stalk still wet, face
Pale as Inca gold,
Spring glistening in every delicate fold.
I knelt down by the roadside there,
Caught the faint whiff of its shy scent
On the cold and public air,
Then got up and went
On my slow way,
Glad and grateful I'd seen
The first primrose that day,
Half yellow, half green.

Leonard Clark

Daffodils

I wandered lonely as a cloud
    That floats on high o'er vales and hills,
When all at once I saw a crowd,
    A host, of golden daffodils;
Beside the lake, beneath the trees,
Fluttering and dancing in the breeze.

Continuous as the stars that shine
    And twinkle on the Milky Way,
They stretched in never-ending line
    Along the margin of a bay:
Ten thousand saw I at a glance,
Tossing their heads in sprightly dance.

The waves beside them danced, but they
    Out-did the sparkling waves in glee:
A poet could not but be gay,
    In such a jocund company:
I gazed – and gazed – but little thought
What wealth the show to me had brought:

For oft, when on my couch I lie
    In vacant or in pensive mood,
They flash upon that inward eye
    Which is the bliss of solitude;
And then my heart with pleasure fills,
And dances with the daffodils.

William Wordsworth

Thistledown

This might have been a place for sleep
But, as from that small hollow there
Hosts of bright thistledown begin
Their dazzling journey through the air,
An idle man can only stare.

They grip their withered edge of stalk
In brief excitement for the wind;
They hold a breathless final talk,
And when their filmy cables part
One almost hears a little cry.

Some cling together while they wait
And droop and gaze and hesitate,
But others leap along the sky,
Or circle round and calmly choose
The gust they know they ought to use.

While some in loving pairs will glide,
Or watch the others as they pass,
Or rest on flowers in the grass,
Or circle through the shining day
Like silvery butterflies at play.

Some catch themselves to every mound,
Then lingeringly and slowly move
As if they knew the precious ground
Were opening for their fertile love:
They almost try to dig, they need
So much to plant their thistle-seed.

Harold Monro

The fairies

Up the airy mountain,
    Down the rushy glen,
We daren't go a-hunting,
    For fear of little men;
Wee folk, good folk,
    Trooping all together;
Green jacket, red cap,
    And white owl's feather!

Down along the rocky shore
    Some make their home,
They live on crispy pancakes
    Of yellow tide-foam;
Some in the reeds
    Of the black mountain-lake
With frogs for their watch-dogs,
    All night awake.

High on the hill-top
    The old King sits;
He is now so old and grey
    He's nigh lost his wits.
With a bridge of white mist
    Columbkill he crosses,
On his stately journeys
    From Slieveleague to Rosses;
Or going up with music
    On cold starry nights,
To sup with the Queen
    Of the gay Northern Lights.

They stole little Bridget
    For seven years long;
When she came down again
    Her friends were all gone.
They took her lightly back,
    Between the night and morrow,
They thought that she was fast asleep
    But she was dead with sorrow.
They have kept her ever since
    Deep within the lakes,
On a bed of flag-leaves,
    Watching till she wakes.

By the craggy hillside,
    Through the mosses bare
They have planted thorn-trees
    For pleasure here and there.
Is any man so daring
    As dig one up in spite,
He shall find the thornies set
    In his bed at night.

Up the airy mountain,
    Down the rushy glen,
We daren't go a-hunting
    For fear of little men;
Wee folk, good folk,
    Trooping all together;
Green jacket, red cap,
    And white owl's feather!

William Allingham

A shooting song

To shoot, to shoot, would be my delight,
To shoot the cats that howl in the night;
To shoot the lion, the wolf, the bear,
To shoot the mad dogs out in the square.

I learnt to shoot with a pop-gun good,
Made out of a branch of elder-wood;
It was round, and long, full half a yard,
The plug was strong, the pellets were hard.

I should like to shoot with a bow of yew,
As the English at Agincourt used to do;
The strings of a thousand bows went twang,
And a thousand arrows whizzed and sang.

117

On Hounslow Heath I should like to ride,
With a great horse-pistol at my side;
It is dark – hark! A robber, I know!
Click! crick-crack! and away we go!

I will shoot with a double-barrelled gun,
Two bullets are better than only one;
I will shoot some rooks to put in a pie;
I will shoot an eagle up in the sky.

I once shot a bandit in a dream,
In a mountain pass I heard a scream,
I rescued the lady, and set her free,
'Do not fear, madam, lean on me!'

With a boomerang I could not aim;
A poison blow-pipe would be the same;
An automatic is my desire,
Get out of the way – one, two, three . . . fire!

William Brighty Rands

The badger

The badger grunting on his woodland track
With shaggy hide and sharp nose scrowed with black
Roots in the bushes and the woods and makes
A great huge burrow in the ferns and brakes
With nose on ground he runs an awkward pace
And anything will beat him in the race
The shepherd's dog will run him to his den
Followed and hooted by the dogs and men
The woodman when the hunting comes about
Goes round at night to stop the foxes out
And hurrying through the bushes ferns and brakes
Nor sees the many holes the badger makes
And often through the bushes to the chin
Breaks the old holes and tumbles headlong in.

When midnight comes a host of dogs and men
Go out and track the badger to his den
And put a sack within the hole and lie
Till the old grunting badger passes by
He comes and hears them let the strongest loose
The old fox hears the noise and drops the goose
The poacher shoots and hurries from the cry
And the old hare half wounded buzzes by
They get a forked stick to bear him down
And clap the dogs and bear him to the town
And bait him all the day with many dogs
And laugh and shout and fright the scampering hogs
He runs along and bites at all he meets
They shout and hollo down the noisy streets.

He turns about to face the loud uproar
And drives the rebels to their very door
The frequent stone is hurled where ere they go
When badgers fight and every one's a foe
The dogs are clapped and urged to join the fray
The badger turns and drives them all away
Though scarcely half as big dimute and small
He fights with dogs for hours and beats them all
The heavy mastiff savage in the fray
Lies down and licks his feet and turns away
The bulldog knows his match and waxes cold
The badger grins and never leaves his hold
He drives the crowd and follows at their heels
And bites them though the drunkard swears and reels.

The frighted women take the boys away
The blackguard laughs and hurries on the fray
He tries to reach the woods an awkward race
But sticks and cudgels quickly stop the chase
He turns again and drives the noisy crowd
And beats the many dogs in noises loud
He drives away and beats them every one
And then they loose them all and set them on
He falls as dead and kicked by boys and men
Then starts and grins and drives the crowd again
Till kicked and torn and beaten out he lies
And leaves his hold and cackles groans and dies.

Some keep a baited badger tame as hog
And tame him till he follows like the dog
They urge him on like dogs and show fair play
He beats and scarcely wounded goes away
Lapped up as if asleep he scorns to fly
And seizes any dog that ventures nigh
Clapped like a dog he never bites the men
But worries dogs and hurries to his den
They let him out and turn a harrow down
And there he fights the host of all the town
He licks the patting hand and tries to play
And never tries to bite or run away
And runs away from noise in hollow trees
Burnt by the boys to get a swarm of bees.

John Clare

The Lincolnshire poacher

When I was bound apprentice, in famous
    Lincolnshire,
Full well I served my master for more than seven year,
Till I took up to poaching, as you shall quickly hear:
Oh, it's my delight on a shining night, in the season of
    the year.

As me and my companion were setting of a snare,
'Twas then we spied the gamekeeper, for him we did
    not care.
For we can wrestle and fight, my boys, and jump out
    anywhere;
Oh, it's my delight on a shining night, in the season of
    the year.

As me and my companions were setting four or five,
And, taking on 'em up again, we caught a hare alive.
We took the hare alive, my boys, and through the
    wood did steer:
Oh, it's my delight on a shining night, in the season of
    the year.

I threw him on my shoulder, and then we trudged on
    home,
We took him to a neighbour's house and sold him for
    a crown,
We sold him for a crown, my boys, but I did not tell
    you where:
Oh, it's my delight on a shining night, in the season of
    the year.

Success to every gentleman that lives in Lincolnshire,
Success to every poacher that wants to sell a hare,
Bad luck to every gamekeeper that will not sell his
    deer:
Oh, it's my delight on a shining night, in the season of
    the year.

Unknown

In a notebook

There was a river overhung with trees
With wooden houses built along in shallows
From which the morning sun drew up a haze
And the gyrations of the early swallows
Paid no attention to the gentle breeze
Which spoke discreetly from the weeping willows.
There was a jetty by the forest clearing
Where a small boat was tugging at its mooring.

And night still lingered underneath the eaves.
In the dark houseboats, families were stirring
And Chinese soup was cooked on charcoal stoves.
Then one by one there came into the clearing
Mothers and daughters bowed beneath their sheaves.
The silent children gathered round me staring
And the shy soldiers setting out for battle
Asked for a cigarette and laughed a little.

From low canoes old men laid out their nets
While on the bank young boys with lines were fishing.
The wicker traps were drawn up by their floats.

124

The girls stood waist-deep in the river washing
Or tossed the day's rice on enamel plates
And I sat drinking bitter coffee wishing
The tide would turn to bring me to my senses
After the pleasant war and the evasive answers.

There was a river overhung with trees.
The girls stood waist deep in the river washing,
And night still lingered underneath the eaves
While on the bank young boys with lines were
     fishing.
Mothers and daughters bowed beneath their sheaves
While I sat drinking bitter coffee wishing –
And the tide turned and brought me to my senses.
The pleasant war brought the unpleasant answers.

The villages are burnt, the cities void;
The morning light has left the river view;
The distant followers have been dismayed;
And I'm afraid, reading this passage now,
That everything I knew has been destroyed
By those whom I admired but never knew;
The laughing soldiers fought to their defeat
And I'm afraid most of my friends are dead.

James Fenton

Our village
(by a villager)

Our village, that's to say not Miss Mitford's village,
    but our village of Bullock Smithy,
Is come into by an avenue of trees, three oak pollards,
    two elders, and a withy;
And in the middle, there's a green of about not
    exceeding an acre and a half;
It's common to all, and fed off by nineteen cows, six
    ponies, three horses, five asses, two foals, seven
    pigs, and a calf!
Besides a pond in the middle, as is held by a similar
    sort of common law lease,
And contains twenty ducks, six drakes, three ganders,
    two dead dogs, four drowned kittens, and twelve
    geese.
Of course the green's cropped very close, and does
    famous for bowling when the little village boys
    play at cricket;
Only some horse, or pig, or cow, or great jackass, is
    sure to come and stand right before the wicket.
There's fifty-five private houses, let alone barns and
    workshops, and pigstyes, and poultry huts, and
    such-like sheds;
With plenty of public-houses – two Foxes, one Green
    Man, three Bunch of Grapes, one Crown, and six
    King's Heads.
The Green Man is reckoned the best, as the only one
    that for love or money can raise
A postilion, a blue jacket, two deplorable lame white
    horses, and a ramshackled 'neat postchaise'.
There's one parish church for all the people, whatsoever
    may be their ranks in life or their degrees.
Except one very damp, small, dark, freezing-cold
    little Methodist chapel of Ease;

And close by the churchyard there's a stone-mason's
        yard, that when the time is seasonable
Will furnish with afflictions sore and marble urns and
        cherubims very low and reasonable.
There's a cage, comfortable enough, I've been in it
        with old Jack Jeffrey and Tom Pike;
For the Green Man next door will send you in ale,
        gin, or anything else you like.
I can't speak of the stocks, as nothing remains of them
        but the upright post;
But the pound is kept in repairs for the sake of Cob's
        horse, as is always there almost.
There's a smithy, of course, where that queer sort of a
        chap in his way, Old Joe Bradley,
Perpetually hammers and stammers, for he stutters
        and shoes horses very badly.
There's a shop of all sorts, that sells everything, kept
        by the widow of Mr Task;
But when you go there, it's ten to one she's out of
        everything you ask.
You'll know her house by the swarm of boys, like
        flies, about the old sugary cask:
There are six empty houses, and not so well papered
        inside as out,
For bill-stickers won't beware, but stick notices of
        sales and election placards all about.
That's the Doctor's with a green door, where the
        garden pots in the windows is seen;
A weakly monthly rose that don't blow, and a dead
        geranium, and a tea-plant with five black leaves
        and one green.
As for hollyoaks at the cottage doors, and honeysuckles
        and jasmines, you may go and whistle;
But the Tailor's front garden grows two cabbages, a
        dock, a ha'porth of pennyroyal, two dandelions,
        and a thistle.

127

There are three small orchards – Mr Busby's the
    schoolmaster's is the chief –
With two pear-trees that don't bear; one plum and an
    apple, that every year is stripped by a thief.
There's another small day-school too, kept by the
    respectable Mrs Gaby.
A select establishment, for six little boys and one big,
    and four little girls and a baby;
There's a rectory, with pointed gables and strange odd
    chimneys that never smoke,
For the rector don't live on his living like other
    Christian sort of folks;
There's a barber's, once a week well filled with rough
    black-bearded shock-headed churls,
And a window with two feminine men's heads, and
    two masculine ladies in false curls;
There's a butcher's, and a carpenter's, and a
    plumber's, and a small greengrocer's and a baker,
But he won't bake on a Sunday, and there's a sexton
    that's a coal-merchant besides, and an
    undertaker;
And a toyshop, but not a whole one, for a village can't
    compare with the London shops;
One window sells drums, dolls, kites, carts, bats,
    Clout's balls, and the other sells malt and hops.
And Mrs Brown, in domestic economy not to be a bit
    behind her betters,
Lets her house to a milliner, a watchmaker, a rat-
    catcher, a cobbler, lives in it herself, and it's the
    post-office for letters.
Now I've gone through all the village – aye, from end
    to end, save and except one more house,
But I haven't come to that – and I hope I never shall –
    and that's the Village Poor House!

Thomas Hood

Miracles
(an extract)

Why, who makes much of a miracle?
As to me I know of nothing else but miracles,
Whether I walk the streets of Manhattan,
Or dart my sight over the roofs of houses toward the
    sky,
Or wade with naked feet along the beach just in the
    edge of the water,
Or stand under trees in the woods,
Or watch honey-bees around the hive of a summer
    forenoon,
Or animals feeding in the fields,
Or birds, or the wonderfulness of insects in the air,
Or the wonderfulness of the sundown, or of the stars
    shining so quiet and bright,
Or the exquisite delicate thin curve of the new moon
    in spring;
These with the rest, one and all, are to me miracles,
The whole referring, yet each distinct and in its place.

To me every hour of the light and dark is a miracle,
Every cubic inch of space is a miracle,
Every square yard of the surface of the earth is spread
    with the same,
Every foot of the interior swarms with the same.

To me the sea is a continual miracle,
The fishes that swim – the rocks – the motion of the
    waves – the ships with men in them,
What stranger miracles are there?

Walt Whitman

The Nightjar

We loved our Nightjar, but she would not stay with
    us.
We had found her lying as dead, but soft and warm,
Under the apple tree beside the old thatched wall.
Two days we kept her in a basket by the fire,
Fed her, and thought she well might live – till
    suddenly
In the very moment of most confiding hope
She raised herself all tense, quivered and drooped and
    died.
Tears sprang into my eyes – why not? the heart of
    man
Soon sets itself to love a living companion,
The more so if by chance it asks some care of him.
And this one had the kind of loveliness that goes
Far deeper than the optic nerve – full fathom five
To the soul's ocean cave, where Wonder and Reason
Tell their alternate dreams of how the world was
    made.
So wonderful she was – her wings the wings of night
But powdered here and there with tiny golden clouds
And wave-line markings like sea-ripples on the sand.
O how I wish I might never forget that bird –
Never!
        But even now, like all beauty of earth,
She is fading from me into the dusk of Time.

Sir Henry Newbolt

The tiger

Tiger! Tiger! burning bright
In the forests of the night,
What immortal hand or eye
Could frame thy fearful symmetry?

In what distant deeps or skies
Burned the fire of thine eyes?
On what wings dare he aspire?
What the hand dare seize the fire?

And what shoulder, and what art,
Could twist the sinews of thy heart?
And when thy heart began to beat,
What dread hand? And what dread feet?

What the hammer? What the chain?
In what furnace was thy brain?
What the anvil? What dread grasp
Dare its deadly terrors clasp?

When the stars threw down their spears,
And watered heaven with their tears,
Did he smile his work to see?
Did he who made the Lamb make thee?

Tiger! Tiger! burning bright
In the forests of the night,
What immortal hand or eye
Dare frame thy fearful symmetry?

William Blake

The donkey

When fishes flew and forests walked
    And figs grew upon thorn,
Some moment when the moon was blood
    Then surely I was born;

With monstrous head and sickening cry
    And ears like errant wings,
The devil's walking parody
    On all four-footed things.

The tattered outlaw of the earth,
    Of ancient crooked will;
Starve, scourge, deride me: I am dumb,
    I keep my secret still.

Fools! For I also had my hour;
    One far fierce hour and sweet:
There was a shout about my ears,
    And palms before my feet.

G. K. Chesterton

The lonely scarecrow

My poor old bones – I've only two –
A broomshank and a broken stave.
My ragged gloves are a disgrace.
My one peg-foot is in the grave.

I wear the labourer's old clothes:
Coat, shirt, and trousers all undone.
I bear my cross upon a hill
In rain and shine, in snow and sun.

I cannot help the way I look.
My funny hat is full of hay.
– O, wild birds, come and nest in me!
Why do you always fly away?

James Kirkup

Mushrooms

Overnight, very
Whitely, discreetly,
Very quietly

Our toes, our noses
Take hold on the loam,
Acquire the air.

Nobody sees us,
Stops us, betrays us;
The small grains make room.

Soft fists insist on
Heaving the needles,
The leafy bedding,

Even the paving.
Our hammers, our rams,
Earless and eyeless,

Perfectly voiceless,
Widen the crannies,
Shoulder through holes. We

Diet on water,
On crumbs of shadow,
Bland-mannered, asking

Little or nothing.
So many of us!
So many of us!

We are shelves, we are
Tables, we are meek,
We are edible,

Nudgers and shovers
In spite of ourselves.
Our kind multiplies:

We shall by morning
Inherit the earth.
Our foot's in the door.

Sylvia Plath

Beautiful Soup

Beautiful Soup, so rich and green,
Waiting in a hot tureen!
Who for such dainties would not stoop?
Soup of the evening, beautiful Soup!
Soup of the evening, beautiful Soup!
      Beau—ootiful Soo—oop!
      Beau—ootiful Soo—oop!
Soo—oop of the e—e—evening,
      Beautiful, beautiful Soup!

Beautiful Soup! Who cares for fish,
Game, or any other dish?
Who would not give all else for two p-
ennyworth only of beautiful Soup?
Pennyworth only of beautiful Soup?
      Beau—ootiful Soo—oop!
      Beau—ootiful Soo—oop!
Soo—oop of the e—e—evening,
      Beau—ti—ful, beauti—FUL SOUP!

Lewis Carroll

The lake isle of Innisfree

I will arise and go now, and go to Innisfree,
And a small cabin build there, of clay and wattles
    made:
Nine bean-rows will I have there, a hive for the
    honey-bee,
And live alone in the bee-loud glade.

And I shall have some peace there, for peace comes
     dropping slow,
Dropping from the veils of the morning to where the
     cricket sings;
There midnight's all a glimmer, and noon a purple
     glow,
And evening full of the linnet's wings.

I will arise and go now, for always night and day
I hear lake water lapping with low sounds by the
     shore;
While I stand on the roadway, or on the pavements
     grey,
I hear it in the deep heart's core.

W. B. Yeats

To autumn

Season of mists and mellow fruitfulness,
     Close bosom-friend of the maturing sun;
Conspiring with him how to load and bless
     With fruit the vines that round the thatch-eaves
         run;
To bend with apples the mossed cottage-trees,
     And fill all fruit with ripeness to the core;
         To swell the gourd, and plump the hazel
           shells
     With a sweet kernel; to set budding more,
And still more, later flowers for the bees,
Until they think warm days will never cease,
         For summer has o'er-brimmed their clammy
           cells.

Who hath not seen thee oft amid thy store?
    Sometimes whoever seeks abroad may find
Thee sitting careless on a granary floor,
    Thy hair soft-lifted by the winnowing wind;
Or on a half-reaped furrow sound asleep,
    Drowsed with the fume of poppies, while thy
        hook
        Spares the next swath and all its twined
          flowers:
And sometimes like a gleaner thou dost keep
    Steady thy laden head across a brook;
    Or by a cider-press, with patient look,
        Thou watchest the last oozings hours by
        hours.

Where are the songs of spring? Ay, where are they?
    Think not of them, thou hast thy music too –
While barred clouds bloom the soft-dying day,
    And touch the stubble-plains with rosy hue;
Then in a wailful choir the small gnats mourn
    Among the river sallows, borne aloft
        Or sinking as the light wind lives or dies;
And full-grown lambs loud bleat from hilly bourn;
    Hedge-crickets sing; and now with treble soft
    The red-breast whistles from a garden-croft;
        And gathering swallows twitter in the skies.

John Keats

Symphony in yellow

An omnibus across the bridge
    Crawls like a yellow butterfly,
    And, here and there, a passer-by
Shows like a little restless midge.

Big barges full of yellow hay
    Are moored against the shadowy wharf,
    And, like a yellow silken scarf,
The thick fog hangs along the quay.

The yellow leaves begin to fade
    And flutter from the Temple elms,
    And at my feet the pale green Thames
Lies like a rod of rippled jade.

Oscar Wilde

The lay of the last minstrel
(an extract)

Breathes there the man, with soul so dead,
Who never to himself hath said,
    This is my own, my native land!
Whose heart hath ne'er within him burned,
As home his footsteps he hath turned,
    From wandering on a foreign strand!
If such there breathe, go, mark him well;
For him no minstrel raptures swell;
High though his titles, proud his name,
Boundless his wealth as wish can claim;
Despite those titles, power, and pelf,
The wretch, concentred all in self,
Living, shall forfeit fair renown,
And, doubly dying, shall go down
To the vile dust, from whence he sprung,
Unwept, unhonoured, and unsung.

O Caledonia! stern and wild,
Meet nurse for a poetic child!
Land of brown heath and shaggy wood,
Land of the mountain and the flood,
Land of my sires! what mortal hand
Can e'er untie the filial band,
That knits me to thy rugged strand!
Still, as I view each well-known scene,
Think what is now, and what hath been,
Seems as, to me, of all bereft,
Sole friends thy woods and streams were left;
And thus I love them better still,
Even in extremity of ill.

By Yarrow's stream still let me stray,
Though none should guide my feeble way;
Still feel the breeze down Ettrick break,
Although it chill my withered cheek;
Still lay my head by Teviot Stone,
Though there, forgotten and alone,
The Bard may draw his parting groan.

Sir Walter Scott

Poem for kids

An old, old man lived down our street
as old as a tortoise with leathery feet

as old as a carp or a minstrel's harp
his eyes were dim but his wits were sharp

he sat and watched the years go by
(perhaps he just *forgot* to die)

he sat and watched the suns go down
no one remembered when his hair was brown

(perhaps it was already white
when Waterloo-men went to fight

perhaps it was as white as frost
when Flodden field was won and lost).

I used to think he was as old
as the first drinking-cups of gold

but his memories lay where they were stored
and he loved the world and he never got bored

and every night when he sank to rest
his dreams were rich, his dreams were blest.

I sometimes wondered why he seemed
so glad with whatever it was he dreamed

and I asked him once, what his dreams were made of?
he answered, *Nothing to be afraid of*:

*Just memories of long-gone days
when the world moved in different ways,*

*just memories of things long gone:
they have passed, but I live on,*

*and so in the dreams inside my head
they will have a home till I am dead.*

And I asked him once if he'd rather be
back when the world moved differently:

I asked him once, but all he would say
was, *Some things go and some things stay,
and the world is a new world every day.*

※

This old man had worked on a ship
and watched the billows swing and skip

in the days when ships held out their sails
to catch the breezes, to dare the gales,

when the engine-room was the windy sky
and the ship drove on with her mast held high

or the ship stood still and the sails hung idle
and skipper and mate were suicidal

till the first sail swelled and the first rope stirred
and the ship came alive like a waking bird:

and there was no coal and there was no oil
just the wind and compass and seamen's toil

and there was no stain and there was no scum
in the harbours where the cargoes come

no dead birds with useless wings
washed up by the tide like forgotten things

only the shove of the salt-sea air
and the cold white horses galloping there.

And I often wondered if he longed to be
afloat again on that sparkling sea

back in those clean and salty days
before the slicks and the greasy haze:

I asked him once, but all he would say,
was, *Some things go and some things stay,*
and the world is a new world every day.

*

Then one day, just before he died,
he took my arm, drew me aside:

yes, just before his spirit passed
he must have thought he'd talk at last.

When I was born I don't remember
but from January to December

in every year that has gone round
since the first man walked on the ground

things were that should never have been
and sights you'd rather not have seen.

No words can ever tell man's story
without some shame, without some glory:

if you go back a thousand years
the picture neither clouds nor clears.

Our kindly earth was not so spoiled,
yet some men lazed, and some men toiled:

some men laughed and some men groaned
and one looked on while another was stoned:

yet there was goodness, too, and boldness,
to set against the greed and coldness.

It's one long tale, without a sequel
and its bad and its good are just about equal:

so what I have to say, young man,
is, Laugh and sing as much as you can:

for some things go, and some things stay,
and the world is a new world every day!

John Wain

Talk

I wish people, when you sit near them,
wouldn't think it necessary to make conversation
and send thin draughts of words
blowing down your neck and your ears
and giving you a cold in your inside.

D. H. Lawrence

Money

When I had money, money, O!
 I knew no joy till I went poor;
For many a false man as a friend
 Came knocking all day at my door.

Then felt I like a child that holds
 A trumpet that he must not blow
Because a man is dead; I dared
 Not speak to let this false world know.

Much have I thought of life, and seen
 How poor men's hearts are ever light;
And how their wives do hum like bees
 About their work from morn till night.

So, when I hear these poor ones laugh,
 And see the rich ones coldly frown –
Poor men, think I, need not go up
 So much as rich men should come down.

When I had money, money, O!
 My many friends proved all untrue;
But now I have no money, O!
 My friends are real, though very few.

      William Henry Davies

Friends

I fear it's very wrong of me,
And yet I must admit,
When someone offers friendship
I want the *whole* of it.
I don't want everybody else
To share my friends with me.
At least, I want *one* special one,
Who, indisputably,

Likes me much more than all the rest,
Who's always on my side,
Who never cares what others say,
Who lets me come and hide
Within his shadow, in his house –
It doesn't matter where –
Who lets me simply be myself,
Who's always, *always* there.

Elizabeth Jennings

The things that matter

Now that I've nearly done my days,
    And grown too stiff to sweep or sew,
I sit and think, till I'm amazed,
    About what lots of things I know:
Things as I've found out one by one –
    And when I'm fast down in the clay,
My knowing things and how they're done
    Will all be lost and thrown away.

148

There's things, I know, as won't be lost,
　　Things as folks write and talk about:
The way to keep your roots from frost,
　　And how to get your ink spots out.
What medicine's good for sores and sprains,
　　What way to salt your butter down,
What charms will cure your different pains,
　　And what will bright your faded gown.

But more important things than these,
　　They can't be written in a book:
How fast to boil your greens and peas,
　　And how good bacon ought to look;
The feel of real good wearing stuff,
　　The kind of apple as will keep,
The look of bread that's rose enough,
　　And how to get a child asleep.

Whether the jam is fit to pot,
　　Whether the milk is going to turn,
Whether a hen will lay or not,
　　Is things as some folks never learn.
I know the weather by the sky,
　　I know what herbs grow in what lane;
And if sick men are going to die,
　　Or if they'll get about again.

Young wives come in, a-smiling, grave,
　　With secrets that they itch to tell:
I know what sort of times they'll have,
　　And if they'll have a boy or gell.
And if a lad is ill to bind,
　　Or some young maid is hard to lead,
I know when you should speak 'em kind,
　　And when it's scolding as they need.

I used to know where birds ud set,
     And likely spots for trout or hare,
And God may want me to forget
     The way to set a line or snare;
But not the way to truss a chick,
     To fry a fish, or baste a roast,
Nor how to tell, when folks are sick,
     What kind of herb will ease them most!

Forgetting seems such silly waste!
     I know so many little things,
And now the angels will make haste
     To dust it all away with wings!
O God, you made me like to know,
     You kept the things straight in my head,
Please God, if you can make it so,
     Let me know *something* when I'm dead.

Edith Nesbit

Song

When I am dead, my dearest,
     Sing no sad songs for me;
Plant thou no roses at my head,
     Nor shady cypress tree:
Be the green grass above me
     With showers and dewdrops wet:
And if thou wilt, remember,
     And if thou wilt, forget.

I shall not see the shadows,
    I shall not feel the rain:
I shall not hear the nightingale
    Sing on as if in pain:
And dreaming through the twilight
    That doth not rise nor set,
Haply I may remember,
    And haply may forget.

Christina Rossetti

The soldier

If I should die, think only this of me:
    That there's some corner of a foreign field
That is for ever England. There shall be
    In that rich earth a richer dust concealed;
A dust whom England bore, shaped, made aware,
    Gave, once, her flowers to love, her ways to
        roam,
A body of England's, breathing English air,
    Washed by the rivers, blest by suns of home.

And think, this heart, all evil shed away,
    A pulse in the eternal mind, no less
        Gives somewhere back the thoughts by
        England given;
Her sights and sounds; dreams happy as her day;
    And laughter, learnt of friends; and gentleness,
        In hearts at peace, under an English heaven.

Rupert Brooke

Upon the hearth the fire is red

Upon the hearth the fire is red,
Beneath the roof there is a bed
But not yet weary are our feet,
Still round the corner we may meet
A sudden tree or standing stone
That none have seen but we alone.

> Tree and flower and leaf and grass,
>   Let them pass! Let them pass!
> Hill and water under sky,
>   Pass them by! Pass them by!

Still round the corner there may wait
A new road or a secret gate,
And though we pass them by today,
Tomorrow we may come this way
And take the hidden paths that run
Towards the moon or to the sun.

> Apple, thorn, and nut and sloe,
>   Let them go! Let them go!
> Sand and stone and pool and dell,
>   Fare you well! Fare you well!

Home is behind, the world ahead,
And there are many paths to tread
Through shadows to the edge of night,
Until the stars are all alight.
Then world behind and home ahead,
We'll wander back to home and bed.

Mist and twilight, cloud and shade,
    Away shall fade! Away shall fade!
Fire and lamp, and meat and bread,
    And then to bed! And then to bed!

J. R. R. Tolkien

Our revels now are ended
(from *The Tempest*)

Our revels now are ended. These our actors,
As I foretold you, were all spirits and
Are melted into air, into thin air:
And, like the baseless fabric of this vision,
The cloud-capped towers, the gorgeous palaces,
The solemn temples, the great globe itself,
Yea, all which it inherit, shall dissolve
And, like this insubstantial pageant faded,
Leave not a rack behind. We are such stuff
As dreams are made on, and our little life
Is rounded with a sleep.

William Shakespeare

Acknowledgments

The editors and publishers wish to thank the following for giving permission to include in this anthology material which is their copyright. If we have inadvertently omitted to acknowledge anyone we should be most grateful if this could be brought to our attention for correction at the first opportunity.

George Allen & Unwin (Publishers) Limited for 'Upon the Hearth the Fire is Red' from *The Road Goes Ever On* by J. R. R. Tolkien.

Associated Book Publishers (UK) Limited (Methuen) and McClelland & Stewart, Toronto, for 'Buckingham Palace' from *When We Were Very Young* by A. A. Milne.

Cassell Limited for 'Warning to Children' from *Collected Poems 1975* by Robert Graves.

The Executors of the W. H. Davies Estate, and Jonathan Cape Limited, for 'Money' from *The Complete Poems of W. H. Davies*.

J. M. Dent & Sons Limited for 'The Donkey' from *The Wild Knight and Other Poems* by G. K. Chesterton.

Dobson Books Limited for 'First Primrose' from *Collected Poems and Verses for Children* by Leonard Clark.

Dodd Mead & Company, New York © 1949, and the Estate of Robert Service, for 'Dunce' from *Collected Verse of Robert Service*.

Gerald Duckworth & Company Limited for 'Matilda – Who Told Lies and Was Burned to Death' from

Cautionary Tales for Children by Hilaire Belloc; and for 'Winter the Huntsman' from *Selected Poems Old and New* by Osbert Sitwell.

Faber and Faber Limited for 'The Night Mail' from *Collected Poems* by W. H. Auden; for 'The Song of the Jellicles' from *Old Possum's Book of Practical Cats* by T. S. Eliot; for 'My Sister Jane' from *Meet My Folks* by Ted Hughes; and for 'Glass Falling' from *The Collected Poems of Louise MacNeice*.

David Higham Associates Limited for 'What Has Happened to Lulu?' from *Collected Poems* by Charles Causley (Macmillan); for 'When Hannibal Crossed the Alps' from *The Children's Bells* by Eleanor Farjeon (Oxford University Press); for 'Friends' from *The Secret Brother* by Elizabeth Jennings (Macmillan); and for 'Johnnie Crack and Flossie Snail' from *Under Milk Wood* by Dylan Thomas (Dent).

Olwyn Hughes for 'Mushrooms' from *The Colossus* by Sylvia Plath (Faber and Faber). © Ted Hughes 1967.

The Executor of the James Joyce Estate, and Jonathan Cape Limited, for 'All Day I Hear the Noise of Waters' from *Chamber Music* by James Joyce.

James Kirkup for his poem 'The Lonely Scarecrow' from his book *A Spring Journey* (Oxford University Press).

Macmillan (London and Basingstoke), and Curtis Brown Limited, for 'Poem for Kids' from *Poems, 1949–1979* by John Wain.

The Literary Trustees of Walter de la Mare and The Society of Authors as their representative for 'The Listeners' and 'Silver' by Walter de la Mare.

John Murray (Publishers) Limited for 'Christmas' and 'Hunter Trials' from *Collected Poems of John Betjeman*; and for 'The Highwayman' from *Collected Poems of Alfred Noyes*.

Peter Newbolt for 'The Nightjar' from *Selected Poems of Henry Newbolt* (Hodder and Stoughton).

Salamander Press, Edinburgh, for 'In a Notebook' from *Memory of War* by James Fenton.

Vernon Scannell for his poem 'Uncle Albert'.

A. P. Watt Limited, The National Trust for Places of Historic Interest or Natural Beauty, and Macmillan London Limited, for 'If' from *The Definitive Edition of Rudyard Kipling's Verse*, and A. P. Watt Limited, Macmillan London, and Michael B. Yeats, for 'The Lake Isle of Innisfree' from *Collected Poems of W. B. Yeats*.

Index of titles

Index of Authors